Abusir

—

Realm of Osiris

Miroslav Verner

Abusir

———

Realm of Osiris

The American University in Cairo Press
Cairo — New York

Copyright © 2002 by
The American University in Cairo Press
113 Sharia Kasr el Aini, Cairo, Egypt
420 Fifth Avenue, New York, NY 10018
www.aucpress.com

An earlier version of this book was published
in the Czech Republic in 1994 under the title
Forgotten Pharaohs, Lost Pyramids: Abusir

Dar el Kutub No. 5359/02
ISBN 977 424 723 X

Designed by
Andrea El-Akshar/AUC Press Design Center

Printed in Jordan

pp. iv – v
Blocks with fine reliefs protruding from the
sand. Revealed recently by Zahi Hawass at
Sahure's causeway (photo: Kamil Voděra).

p. vi
Princess Khekeretnebty looking on as her
funerary offerings are brought to her. Mastaba
of Khekeretnebty. Wall painting. End of the
Fifth Dynasty. Abusir (photo: Kamil Voděra).

In Egyptian they called it Per Usir, "the Realm of Osiris".

The Greeks took this into their language as Busiris,

which led to the Arabic name of Abusir.

Contents

	Preface	1
CHAPTER I	In the Shadow of Memphis	5
CHAPTER II	Abusir—the Rise of a Royal Necropolis	41
CHAPTER III	Under the Sign of the Sun	67
CHAPTER IV	The Royal Mother	89
CHAPTER V	The Secret of the Unfinished Pyramid	111
CHAPTER VI	The Testimony of the Papyrus Archives	134
CHAPTER VII	The Dazzling Career of the Royal Hairdresser	153
CHAPTER VIII	The Traitor's Tomb?	177
CHAPTER IX	Iufaa—an Intact Tomb!	193
CHAPTER X	South Abusir: at the Crossroads of History	207
CHAPTER XI	In Search of Lost Time	225
	Chronological List of Rulers and Dynasties	239
	Select Bibliography	243
	Index	245

Preface

In Egypt today there are several dozen villages called Abusir. Only one of them, however, can boast of being an archaeological site of the first importance: this is the Abusir near which lies a cemetery dominated by the pyramids of the Fifth Dynasty pharaohs. But, though situated in the very center of the renowned pyramid fields of the Memphite necropolis, Abusir has always remained at the periphery of archaeological interest and in the shadow of its more famous neighbors Saqqara and Giza. This lack of interest has undoubtedly contributed to the lamentable state of the major monuments of the Abusir cemetery—the pyramids of the Fifth Dynasty kings. Their casings ripped away, their cores crumbling, and plundered for centuries by thieves searching for treasure, or at least rare kinds of stone, the pyramids of Abusir today resemble uninviting heaps of stone. Perhaps another factor contributing to the waning of interest in Abusir was the impact of excavations carried out in the first years of this century by a German archaeological expedition. The breadth of these excavations and their outstanding quality for the period seemed to pre-empt further efforts. The Germans' brilliant, and rapidly published, results contributed to the spread of the idea that everything of archaeological importance and interest in the locality had already been thoroughly investigated.

Nevertheless, the results of the first Czech Egyptological project at Abusir, which began forty years ago and involved excavations in the area of the great tomb of the Vizier Ptashepses, were to indicate that the site had not yet yielded up all its secrets.

Now, the ongoing Czech excavations in Abusir are fundamentally extending and modifying our archaeological picture of the locality. Previously unknown pyramids,

Alabaster offering table of Queen Udjebten near the southeastern corner of the pyramid of Pepi II in South Saqqara (photo: Milan Zemina).

temples, tombs, and even entire large cemeteries, all dating from different periods of Egyptian history, have been discovered. Newly discovered papyri from the Abusir temple archives have been deposited in the vaults of the Egyptian Museum at Cairo, and the most interesting and valuable archaeological finds from the new Abusir excavations have been exhibited at selected Egyptian museums. Research papers drawing on the newly discovered archaeological and epigraphic sources have also been multiplying. It is no exaggeration to say that the excavations in Abusir have become one of those archaeological works in Egypt which are carefully followed by the scholarly public.

The first edition of this book, named *Forgotten Pharaohs, Lost Pyramids: Abusir*, published in 1994, has already been sold out. Moreover, a series of important new discoveries made by the Czech archaeological team in Abusir in recent years—especially, in Neferefre's pyramid, Iufaa's shaft tomb and the South Abusir cemetery—have made a new edition of the book urgent. Largely reworked and updated, the book is now published by the American University in Cairo Press under the title *Abusir: Realm of Osiris*. It is the author's wish and hope that this book will become one of the pieces of the once lost but progressively rediscovered mosaic of the history of the royal cemetery at Abusir.

This book could never have been written without the support of leading representatives of Egypt's Supreme Council of Antiquities and without the unstinting cooperation of Egyptian colleagues and friends in the Giza and Saqqara Antiquities Inspectorates. The author is also much obliged to colleagues in the Egyptian Museum in Cairo for permission to photograph and publish some of the museum's masterpieces. To all these friends I offer much-deserved thanks.

The Preface and Chapters I, III–VIII and XI were translated by Dr. Anna Bryson and Jana Klepetářová, the remaining parts of the text by the author of the book himself.

In preparing the revised edition of this book, I am indebted to Dr. Vivienne G. Callender for supervision of the English text, to Eng. Jolana Malátková and Eng. Luděk Wellner for the line drawings, Milan Zemina and Kamil Voděra for the majority of the photographs, to Dr. Jaromír Krejčí for CAD images of the Abusir pyramid field and some architectonic details from Neferefre's pyramid and, eventually, to Mgr. Hana Vymazalová for help in the photo-archive of the Czech Institute of Egyptology. To all—sincere thanks.

Miroslav Verner

Prague, 30th August 2001

Alabaster sphinx (Amenhotep II ?) that originally adorned the southern approach to the Temple of Ptah. Mit Rahina (photo: Milan Zemina).

CHAPTER I

In the Shadow of Memphis

F looded with sunlight, the landscape of the Nile Valley is a network of irrigation canals interwoven with a many-colored mosaic of fields, villages, gardens, and palm groves. The area around the village of Mit Rahina, not far from the famous Step Pyramid at Saqqara, is no exception. At first sight there is almost nothing to suggest that it was here, almost within sight of the high-rise buildings of Cairo, which encroach ever campaigns to the Western Asia. It was a city which, at the height of its prosperity, extended over an area of approximately 50 square kilometers, but which then vanished almost without trace. The efforts of the archaeologists who have been attempting to unearth its secrets since the beginning of the last century resemble in some ways the proverbial drop in the ocean but have nevertheless continued to bring us new discoveries and new knowledge. The history of the magnificent city has not been lost forever.

Meni, the legendary unifier of Egypt and founder of the First Dynasty, who is credited with the founding of Memphis, could scarcely have chosen a more suitable site on which to build an administrative center for the newly established state. He selected a place on the southern bank of the Nile near the point at which the river valley spreads out into its delta. Just a few kilometers to the north, the Nile, whose course has shifted three kilometers east over the last five thousand years, divides into the branches that determine the basic shape of the Delta. To the east and west the narrow, rocky banked valley, is surrounded by the immense desert. The city which Meni founded was called *Ineb(u) hedj*, "The White Wall(s)," perhaps because the ramparts of the stronghold which at the same time served as the royal residence, were white.

For the ancient Egyptians, the date palm, shown here almost ready to harvest, was a symbol of peace and fertility (photo: Kamil Voděra)

The god Ptah, Lord of Memphis. Detail of sunk relief from the so-called Small Temple of Ptah of Ramesses II. Kom al-Rabia'a, Mit Rahina (photo: Milan Zemina).

Ruins of the Columned Hall of the Temple of Ptah, Mit Rahina (photo: Milan Zemina).

The precise site of this historic center of Memphis has not yet been located with any certainty, although the latest British archaeological researches, using deep-hole drilling, have indicated that it could lie under the northern part of the present-day village of Mit Rahina. At any rate, the remains of "the White Wall" and of later Memphis, lie under several meters of Nile mud.

It is believed that, in addition to the stronghold, Meni also founded a temple of Ptah, the chief god of the new royal seat. Judging by Ptah's epithet "who-is-south-of-his-wall," the temple was probably built south of the stronghold "White Wall(s)." Some archaeological finds indicate that the remnants of the early Temple of Ptah may lay under the houses built on a hillock called Kom al-Fakhry. The temple, which gradually became one of the greatest in the land, was called *Hutkaptah*, "The Temple of the Spirit of Ptah," and in the later pronunciation *Hikupta*. In its garbled and Graecized form it was the origin of the name Egypt itself. It seems that every Egyptian ruler considered it an obligation to extend and augment the Temple of Ptah with his own buildings, statues, obelisks and other features. As in the case of the Temple of Amon in Karnak, so in Memphis there gradually emerged an enormous temple complex of which only a small part has so far been uncovered and archaeologically investigated. For much information about the Temple of Ptah at Memphis we are indebted to the Greek historian Herodotus, who may have actually visited it in the mid-fifth century BCE. The ancient Egyptians regarded the god Ptah as the god-creator and the patron of craftsmen and artisans. Ptah with his wife, the lion goddess Sakhmet, and his son Nefertem, formed what is called the Divine Triad of Memphis. Later a complete Memphite religious doctrine developed which concerned the creation of the world on the basis of Ptah.

A major contribution to the development of the Temple of Ptah was made by Ramesses II, from whose reign date a number of the parts of the building that have so far been uncovered. These include the hypostyle hall and the South Gate, on which colossal statues of the pharaoh once stood accompanied by other figures. Work on extending the Temple of Ptah proceeded into the Ptolemaic Dynasty. Besides Ptah and his triad, other deities were worshipped in Memphis, first among them being Hathor, the goddess of love and beauty and the guardian of the family. There were also non-Egyptian deities, whose cults were practiced by the numerous foreigners living in Memphis. One important Memphis deity was the sacred bull Apis, regarded as the earthly incarnation of the god Ptah. His temple has not yet been discovered, but a building in which embalming and mummification ceremonies were carried out on the sacred bulls has been found. Enormous alabaster embalming tables decorated with lion figures were found within it. The mummies of the sacred bulls were buried not far away, in North Saqqara, in the underground catacombs of the Serapeum, which was once linked with Memphis by means of an alley of sphinxes.

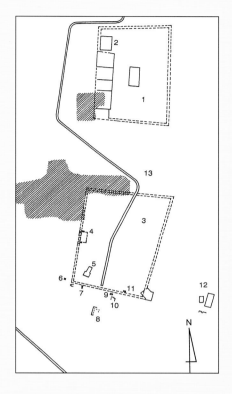

Plan of the parts of ancient Memphis so far archaeologically investigated.
1. Northern Enclosure;
2. Palace of Apries; Enclosure of Ptah;
4. Pylon and hypostyle hall;
5. Embalming house of Apis-bulls;
6. Tombs of high-priests of Memphis;
7. Temple of Ramesses II;
8. Temple of Hathor;
9. Colossus of Ramesses II;
10. Temple of Ramesses II;
11. Alabaster Sphinx (perhaps of Amenhotep II);
12. Palace of Merenptah.

Ruins of the Palace of Apries from the Twenty-sixth Dynasty. Mit Rahina (photo: Milan Zemina).

The district of the Temple of Ptah constituted the southern center of Memphis. A second center, a few kilometers to the north, was later formed around the district of the Palace of Apries. Apries, the Egyptian equivalent of the Greek name pronounced "Haaibre," was a relatively powerful pharaoh of the Twenty-sixth Dynasty. He built a fort in Memphis that had a rectangular ground plan and a massive enclosure wall. He constructed a large palace at the northeast corner of the fort on a raised platform. The platform, the major part of the other buildings making up the Apries Palace, and the fort were all built out of mud bricks. It is possible that this building material, which at the time of the destruction of the monuments attracted less interest than did the various kinds of stone, contributed to the survival of the ruins of the Apries Palace, which were preserved up to a height of approximately ten meters. The mound of the Palace ruins is now the highest place in Memphis. Looking westward from the top of the mound the view is a unique panorama of the Memphite necropolis and the pyramids that dominate it.

Opposite:
Alabaster embalming table. The so-called Embalming House of the Sacred Apis Bulls from the reign of Sheshonq I. Mit Rahina (photo: Milan Zemina).

From ancient Egyptian written material we know that Memphis was the capital of Egypt throughout the entire period of the Old Kingdom, i.e. almost to the end of the third millennium BCE. It was even, briefly (in the period after the collapse of Akhnaten's experiment in reform) the capital in the New Kingdom. Even in the periods when it was not the capital city, Memphis maintained its status as an important administrative and religious center, especially for the northern and central parts of the country. It continued to be the biggest city in Egypt. Its fame only dwindled con-

View of Kom al-Fakhry. The older part of the complex of the Temple of Ptah is believed to lie under this hill. Mit Rahina (photo: Milan Zemina).

Following pages: Hathor capital. Temple of the Goddess Hathor built by Ramesses II. Kom al-Rabia'a, Mit Rahina (photo: Milan Zemina).

clusively in the first centuries CE when the half-crumbled and deserted temples and palaces of Memphis were transformed into a large quarry from which building material could be obtained cheaply. After the occupation of Egypt by the army of Amr Ibn al-Aas in 641, the fortress of Fustat was built from the ruins of Memphis on the site of the fallen Byzantine stronghold Babylon, a place that was later to be the site of a new capital city: Cairo.

Research has made it possible to identify more than a hundred archaeological locations in the area covered by ancient Memphis. So far, the oldest antiquities uncovered are the remains of a residential area and artisans' workshops dating from as early as the First Intermediate Period and beginning of the Middle Kingdom. They were discovered near Kom al-Fakhry. It has not proved possible to find monuments from the third millennium BCE yet, although there must once have been a very large number of these. The Old Kingdom, after all, which was the "era of the pyramid-builders," was the age of the greatest flowering of Memphis.

The monuments, undoubtedly very diverse, were located at city sites which were often quite distant from one another. Attached to them were groups of administrative and residential buildings, which, despite their peripheral position, were very important. These grew up in the vicinity of the valley temples of the royal pyramid complexes on the edge of the desert. Some of these so-called "pyramid towns" temporarily acquired extraordinary importance. One example is the pyramid town near the valley temple of Teti, first ruler of the Sixth Dynasty, in North Saqqara. Insofar as its position was concerned it was just a suburb a few kilometers from the Temple of Ptah, but for a certain time during the first Intermediate Period it became the politico-administrative center of Egypt. Similarly, it is believed that at the end of the Sixth Dynasty and especially at the beginning of the Middle Kingdom, importance was acquired by that part of the capital which spread out to the environs of the valley temple of Pepi I, in what today is South Saqqara. The pyramid complex of Pepi I was called *Men-nefer-Pepi*, "The beauty of Pepi is enduring." The shortened form of this name, *Men-nefer*, Memphis" in Greek, began to be used to designate the whole capital city from the time of the Middle Kingdom. It is somehow fitting that it was a pyramid which gave the oldest of Egypt's capital cities its name. The destiny of Memphis—its rise, flowering, and glory—was inextricably linked to the pyramids and the cemeteries lying at their feet. This relationship was aptly

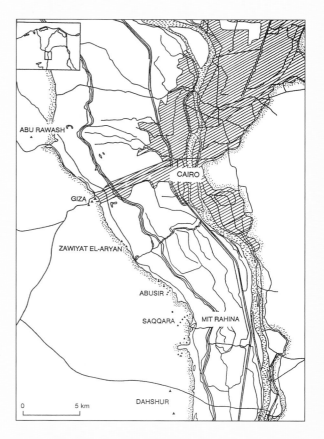

expressed by the Belgian Egyptologists Jean Capart and Marcelle Werbrouck when, in 1930, they entitled their book on the oldest capital of Egypt at the period of its greatest flowering, *Memphis a l'ombre des pyramides*—"Memphis in the Shadow of the Pyramids."

The royal pyramid cemeteries of former Memphis lie like a string of pearls along the western edge of the Nile valley from the borders of today's Cairo in the north right down to Meidum at the entrance to the Fayyum oasis in the south. Here, in the places where the sun set and where the limitless desert from which there was no return began, lay the land of the dead—the empire of the god Osiris. The reasons why the ancient Egyptians buried their dead on the edge of the desert on the western bank of the Nile are evident enough. The same, however, cannot be said of the reasons for their particular choice of sites for pyramid-building. Why, for example, did the founder of the Fourth Dynasty, Sneferu, build his first pyramid at Meidum and then abandon the place, building another two of his pyramids approximately 50 kilometers further north at Dahshur? Why did his son Khufu build his tomb, the celebrated Great Pyramid, still further to the north, in Giza? Why did

Map showing the pyramid cemeteries of ancient Memphis.

the last ruler of the Fourth Dynasty, Shepseskaf, forsake the royal cemetery at Giza and, once again, select for his tomb a faraway site in a deserted spot at South Saqqara? The questions are numerous and, as a rule, answers to them remain on the level of conjecture.

Some Egyptologists believe that the choice of site for the construction of pyramids was determined by the very practical consideration of proximity to limestone quar-

ries, since this type of stone was the basic building material. The limestone in question was the lower-quality limestone which was to be found on the western bank of the Nile and was used particularly for the so-called core of the pyramid, in contrast to the exterior casing for which it was necessary to transport fine white limestone all the way from the quarries in the hills of Moqattam on the opposite, eastern, bank of the Nile. There is certainly some force to this theory. After all, limestone quarries have been discovered near many pyramids. Nevertheless, limestone occurs almost everywhere in the area of the Memphite necropolis and the technical difficulties involved in obtaining it and transporting it to the building site did not vary substantially between the different places.

There is an alternative and quite widespread opinion which was first expressed some time ago by the German Egyptologist Adolf Erman. In Erman's view, a pyramid would be built in the vicinity of a pharaoh's residence, the location of which could change. Although the offices of the highest organs of state, including the royal palace, were situated in Memphis, the rulers would build their other residences outside the capital city, often with a view to some pressing political, economic, or military interests. One particular variant, or addition, to the Erman theory is represented by the opinion that a ruler would deliberately build his palace near the building site of his pyramid with the aim of being present and personally participating in decisions on the serious organizational matters of the greatest and most important state project of his time—the building of the pyramid. Unfortunately, even in the case of Erman's theory, we are dealing with pure conjecture, since so far we have not managed to discover and archaeologically investigate a single one of the royal residences of the Old Kingdom.

The Early Dynastic royal cemetery in North Saqqara is the oldest in the Memphite

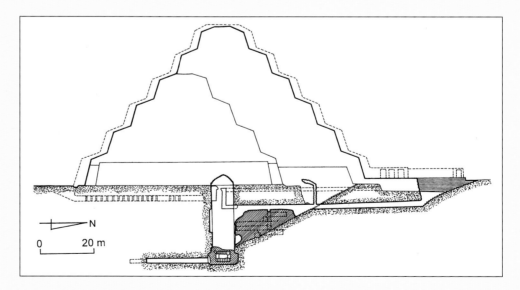

North–south section of the Step Pyramid (by J-Ph. Lauer).

necropolis. The British Egyptologist Walter Brian Emery, who carried out excavations there for many years, believed that the first rulers of a united Egypt, whose seat Memphis had become, were interred in this cemetery. His view, however, did not make headway and the prevailing view among Egyptologists now is that the first rulers of a united Egypt, the pharaohs of the First Dynasty, were still being buried in the old royal cemetery of Upper Egypt at Abydos, at the place which natives of the region today call Umm al-Qaab, "Mother of Potsherds." They believe that the tombs in the Early Dynastic cemetery in North Saqqara are either cenotaphs, false tombs constructed as a symbol of a ruler's presence close to the new capital of the united Egypt, or, more probably, that they are the tombs of the highest state officials and members of the royal family who held posts in Memphis. The Early Dynastic tombs in Saqqara have the form of mastabas (from the Arabic—"mastaba," an elongated rectangular clay bench) of large dimensions. They were built out of mud bricks and the outer surfaces of their walls, decorated with niches, were brightly painted to resemble the original model, which was of wooden poles and matting. The remains of rich burial equipment have been discovered in the underground chambers of several of these tombs.

The Step Pyramid, Saqqara (photo: Milan Zemina).

The monumental gate of Djoser's pyramid complex, Saqqara (photo: Milan Zemina).

The tombs of the rulers of the Second Dynasty, which for the most part have not yet been discovered, represent one of the greatest problems of Egyptian archaeology. It is believed that the majority of these were located in the Saqqara cemetery near the Step Pyramid. Two enormous underground galleries discovered to the north of the Step Pyramid's enclosure wall are considered to be the underground section of the tombs of the second Dynasty kings. The period during which this dynasty governed was unsettled and the stability of united Egypt was extremely fragile. There was probably even a breakdown in the unity of the country with consequent internal conflicts and the despoiling of the royal cemetery in Saqqara. Stabilization of conditions was only achieved by the last Second Dynasty ruler Khasekhemwy. His tomb lies in Abydos, but one of the two already mentioned underground galleries discovered south of the Step Pyramid at Saqqara is also attributed to him.

The beginning of the Third Dynasty brought a fundamental change in the design of royal tombs. As a result, the appearance of the royal cemeteries to the south of Memphis underwent a basic change. The founder of the dynasty, Netjerikhet, later called Djoser, built his tomb in the Saqqara cemetery not far from the underground galleries of his predecessors of the Second Dynasty. Originally the tomb took the form of a mastaba of relatively modest dimensions. In subsequent building phases, however, it was extended and remodeled as a six-stepped pyramid more than 60 meters in height and the first monument of its type. The architect of the Step Pyramid, as well as a a whole complex of other buildings of symbolic religious and cult significance, was Imhotep, who was probably Djoser's son. Later generations venerated him as a sage and the son of the god Ptah. On an area 545 meters by 278 Imhotep created a symbolic residence for the dead king, from which rose the Step Pyramid—a gigantic stairway by which Djoser's spirit would make its way heavenward. The whole complex of buildings, including a high enclosure wall, was built of shining white limestone. The pyramid could be seen from a great distance and was more than just a tomb: it was the visible expression of the pharaoh's power. The Step Pyramid complex in Saqqara, which is considered the oldest work of monumental stone architecture in the world, became a great source of inspiration to Djoser's successors. They too started to build their tombs in the form of pyramids. His immediate heirs, the rulers of the Third Dynasty, also built step pyramids. Djoser's successor, Sekhemkhet, although he did not complete the task, began to build his tomb immediately next to the Step Pyramid. Also unfinished was the pyramid of Khaba, who abandoned the cemetery in Saqqara and chose for his pyramid a place only a few kilometers to the north and close to what is today the village of Zawiyet al-Aryan. The tombs of the remaining few rulers of the Third Dynasty have yet to be discovered.

The last pyramid to be designed and built in step form (except for the original plan

Lake and pyramids (Sneferu's Red and Amenemhet III's) at Dahshur viewed from the southeast (photo: Milan Zemina).

The Red Pyramid, Dahshur (photo: Milan Zemina).

of Neferirkare's pyramid of the Fifth Dynasty at Abusir) lies approximately 60 kilometers to the east of Saqqara near the modern village of Meidum. The last ruler of the Third Dynasty, Huni, has sometimes been credited with initiating the building but archaeological finds have shown that it was the work of the Fourth Dynasty ruler Sneferu. Sneferu probably selected the site for the pyramid with a view to its strategic significance in the Nile valley near to the entrance to the Fayyum Oasis. The pyramid was built first in seven and later in eight steps. For reasons that are not quite clear (perhaps the retreat of the astral and the coming of the solar religion) it was decided to change it into what is called a true pyramid. Sneferu, however, was never buried in this pyramid, even though a large cemetery with the tombs of members of the ruling family was established around it. The German-American physicist Kurt Mendelssohn was inspired by a visit to Meidum and a view of the peculiar configuration of the ruins of the pyramid to formulate an interesting theory. According to Mendelssohn a catastrophe must have occurred during the final stage of building. In the construction of the external casing, in other words during the conversion of the step pyramid into a true pyramid, erroneous calculations and faulty binding of the limestone blocks caused what is known as a "flowing effect" and the ultimate collapse of the pyramid's external casing. Although this theory sounds quite seductive, archaeologists have now rejected it and shown that the pyramid at Meidum, like many others, was gradually destroyed by people quarrying it for stone over centuries.

The reasons that led Sneferu to abandon the pyramid, together with the residence and the town in its neighborhood, have not yet been explained. He chose a new site for pyramid construction approximately 50 kilometers further north and near modern Dahshur. The pyramid that he decided to build in Dahshur was from the very beginning designed as a true pyramid. The chosen angle of inclination of the pyramid walls—60°—proved in the course of construction to be too steep. At the same time, the base on which the pyramid was built was not very stable. The problem was that the foundation was not rock but a compact gravel and sand layer which was unable to bear the pressure of the increasing mass of the pyramid. The walls of the rooms in the heart of the pyramid began to crack. For this reason it was decided to reduce the angle of inclination in the upper part of the pyramid and so considerably lessen the pressure on the inner chambers. As a result of this experimentation and improvisation the pyramid is today called the Bent or sometimes the Rhomboidal or Two-Slope Pyramid. It is unique among pyramids not only for its shape but also for its two entrances, from the north and the west, and the very unusual layout of its inner rooms.

It was undoubtedly as a result of the complications during the construction of the Bent Pyramid and in view of the impaired stability of its inner chambers that work

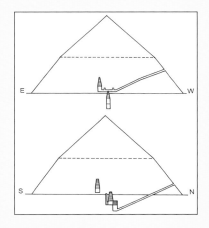

North–south and east–west section of the Bent Pyramid (by A. Fakhry).

Following pages:
The Bent Pyramid. Dahshur (photo: Milan Zemina).

was started, a little further way away, on building another pyramid for Sneferu with a relatively small angle of inclination for the outer wall. This is today named the Red Pyramid after the color of the stone from which it was built. It was in this pyramid that Sneferu was probably buried. In the environs of both of the Dahshur pyramids a new cemetery was established containing the tombs of other members of the royal family and high state officials.

It seems incredible that Sneferu had yet another pyramid built, although this was much smaller than the preceding ones. It stands in Seila, perhaps ten kilometers west of the Meidum pyramid, on a small hill overlooking the depression of the Fayyum Oasis. This pyramid had no inner or underground chambers and was not planned as a tomb but probably simply as a symbol of royal power. The total volume of masonry for all of Sneferu's pyramids amounts to approximately 3.6 million cubic meters, a building record which none of the Egyptian pharaohs were ever to overtake. The technical, organizational, and administrative significance of this figure can be fully grasped only when we remember that in Sneferu's time the whole of Egypt from the Mediterranean Sea to the first Nile cataract at Aswan had no more that one to one and a half million inhabitants.

View of the pyramids at Giza from the southeast (photo: Milan Zemina).

Whether because Dahshur was no longer a suitable place to build further great pyramids or because the local limestone quarries did not meet requirements, or for other reasons, Sneferu's son Khufu (Gr. Cheops) decided to found a new cemetery at Giza, perhaps 30 kilometers north from Dahshur. The site selected consisted of a rocky area of the easternmost promontory of the Libyan Desert above the Nile Valley just where it begins to spread out into the broad delta. Khufu's pyramid measured about 230.4 meters along each side of its square base. With a wall gradient of 51°50′35″ it reached a height of 146.50 meters. It is the largest of the Egyptian pyramids and is justly called the Great Pyramid and one of the Seven Wonders of the World. Its unique system of internal chambers, especially the so-called Great Gallery and King's Chamber is, from the point of view of construction one of the most ingenious ever created in Ancient Egypt. In volume the Great Pyramid is approximately 2.5 million cubic meters. Until recently it was believed that it was built with limestone quarried from the rocky massif near the site. The latest geophysical researches—carried out by French scientists—have shown, however, that the core of the Great Pyramid probably consists of solid stone masonry combined with a system of chambers constructed from stone blocks and filled with sand and rubble. This method was not only very economical and time-saving but also helped to increase the stability of the Great Pyramid during the earthquakes which occasionally occur in Egypt. A number of other buildings were components of Khufu's tomb and together with the pyramid made up an integrated whole: the valley temple (recently discovered by the Egyptian archaeologist Zahi Hawass but not yet fully investigated), the causeway, the mortuary temple at the eastern foot of the pyramid (today almost nothing remains of this except remnants of paving), the small cult pyramid, five pits for the symbolic burial of boats (one of the two boats which were preserved was raised in 1954) and the three small pyramids of the queens.

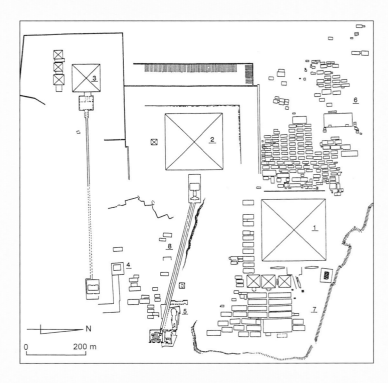

Plan of the Giza necropolis (by G.A. Reisner).

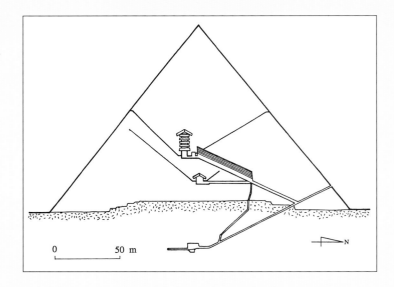

North–south section of the Great Pyramid.

Opposite: Irrigation canal near Giza (photo: Milan Zemina).

This page clockwise: The rock-cut tomb of Kakherptah on the eastern edge of the East Cemetery. Fifth Dynasty, Giza (photo: Milan Zemina).

The pillared hall of Chephren's valley temple, Giza (photo: Milan Zemina).

The ruins of Djedefre's pyramid (prior to the Swiss-French excavation), Abu Rawash (photo: Milan Zemina).

Khufu's son and heir Djedefre abandoned the cemetery established by his father and started to build his pyramid complex approximately seven kilometers further north, by modern Abu Rawash. Archaeological finds of numerous fragments of statues of Djedefre, heaped in the pit for the funerary boat, supported the idea that the tomb had been deliberately destroyed as an expression of religio-politically motivated conflict within the ruling house. This theory has, however, been rejected in recent times.

Another of Khufu's sons, Khafre (Gr. Chephren), who ascended the throne after Radjedef, returned to Giza. His tomb almost achieved the heights of his father's pyramid. The complex of buildings belonging to it likewise recalled his father's monument in its basic characteristics. In Khafre's pyramid complex the valley temple remains in very good condition, relative to other structures of the same age, and today it is considered another of the supreme works of ancient Egyptian architecture. In this temple, built out of enormous blocks of limestone and red granite, discoveries have included a seated diorite statue of Khafre with the falcon god, Horus, shielding his head from behind with outspread wings. Today, this statue is one of the most famous exhibits in the Egyptian Museum in Cairo. The Great Sphinx, the lion deity with the human head symbolically guarding not only the ruler's pyramid complex but the whole Giza cemetery, is also part of the Khafre complex.

The third and smallest pyramid was built in Giza by Khafre's son Menkaure (Gr. Mykerinos). Despite the much smaller dimensions of his pyramid, Menkaure failed to complete the whole complex of buildings making up the tomb, and including the three small pyramids for the queens, during his own lifetime. This was accomplished by his successor Shepseskaf. Nevertheless, during excavations at the Menkaure pyramid complex an American archaeological expedition, led by George Andrew Reisner, managed to find what is so far the largest group of Old Kingdom royal statues yet recovered. These masterpieces of ancient Egyptian sculpture are today on permanent exhibition in museums in Cairo and Boston.

Just as the members of the ruler's family and the highest state officials lived their lives in the proximity of their lord and god, so they wished to rest in the shadow of his pyramid and to enjoy his favor and protection even after death. Similarly the Pharaoh himself wished to be forever surrounded by his court, his relatives, and his officials. Thus around the pyramids at Giza—as before in Saqqara, Meidum, and Dahshur—large cemeteries of private tombs grew up. Many of these tombs, and especially those in the vicinity of the pyramid of Cheops, have been excavated by the Reisner expedition, an Austrian expedition led by Hermann Junker, an Egyptian expedition led by Selim Hassan, and others. In the so-called Western Field to the west of the pyramid of Khufu lie the tombs of the ruler's courtiers, among them the biggest of the Giza mastabas, G2000, unfortunately anonymous and only identified by a number on the archaeological plan of the cemetery. Later tombs are also located here; for example that of the famous Senedjemib Inty, vizier and royal builder from the reign of Djedkare. In the Eastern Field, again in rows, are the equally large mastabas of the highest-ranking members of the royal family; for example prince Ankhhaf, vizier in the reign of Khafre, whose celebrated and splendid bust is today exhibited in the museum in Boston. Also to be found in a dominant position here is the mastaba of Khufukhaf, which perhaps belonged to none other than the future pharaoh Khafre before he became king and changed the element "Khufu" (his father's name) in his own name to Re, the name of the sun god. Members of the royal family, courtiers, and officials from the reign of Khafre were buried in the Central Field, in the central part of the Giza cemetery south of the causeway leading from the valley to the pharaoh's pyramid. A rather small cemetery, established in the reign of Menkaure, consists of mastabas and rock-cut tombs lying in an area of former quarries southeast of the pharaoh's pyramid.

Detail of a statue of the pharaoh Khafre, his head shielded from behind by the outstretched wings of the falcon god Horus. Diorite, 168 centimeters in height. Found in 1860 in the pharaoh's valley temple at Giza by the French archaeologist Auguste Mariette. The statue is now one of the most famous exhibits of the Egyptian Museum in Cairo (no. CG 14) (photo: Milan Zemina).

The Great Sphinx with Khafre's pyramid in the background, Giza (photo: Milan Zemina).

Despite long years of intensive archaeological researches and excavations, however, the royal pyramid cemetery in Giza is still far from fully explored, a fact amply borne out by the surprising discoveries in the area south of the Menkaure valley temple. Here, on the hillside and at the foot of the escarpment, the Egyptian archaeologist Zahi Hawass found a cemetery with the tombs of artisans who had built the royal pyramids. Not far from here, the American archaeologist Mark Lehner discovered extensive mud brick structures of an economic character—the "provisioning section" of the builders of the Giza pyramids including great storehouses for grain and drink, bakeries, and so on. Another important discovery was made by Zahi Hawass in front of Khafre's valley temple where the remnants of foundation of structures, including two "tunnels" dug through the bedrock, were revealed. The structures, built originally of lightweight plant materials and mudbrick, appear to have been the remnants of a large harbor and buildings occasionally used for Khafre's burial ceremonies.

After the death of Menkaure, there were complications in the country's internal political situation. The building of gigantic pyramids had drained off major material resources and the mortuary cults had tied up much of the labor force and finances; it was a situation that could not but have a negative effect on economic conditions in the country. The situation was probably further complicated by succession disputes within the royal family and by the growing importance of the solar cult. This is the

The Mastabat Fara'un, south Saqqara (photo: Milan Zemina).

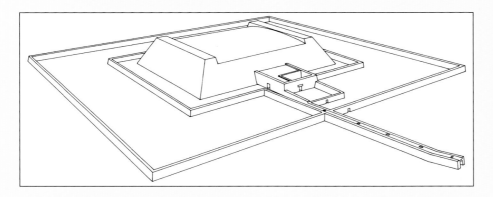

Reconstruction of the original appearance of Shepseskaf's tomb complex (by H. Ricke).

historical background against which we must interpret the decision of the last Fourth Dynasty ruler, Shepseskaf, to build himself a tomb several kilometers to the south of Giza, in South Saqqara. He did not build it in the form of a pyramid, as was usual for pharaohs at the time, but as a mastaba and, what is more, a mastaba resembling a large sarcophagus. The natives call it Mastabat Fara'un, the "Pharaoh's bench." In comparison with the pyramids of Shepseskaf's predecessors, it was a very small and relatively modest tomb. Its unusual design has led Egyptologists to speculate whether it did not represent Shepseskaf's deliberate religiously-motivated renunciation of the pyramid shape, so intimately linked with the solar cult (which was ultimately to prevail with the accession of the Fifth Dynasty), and thus a protest against the growing power of the priests of the sun god Re.

Userkaf, Shepseskaf's successor and the first Fifth Dynasty ruler, did not abandon Saqqara; nevertheless he had his tomb, again in pyramid form, built within the area of the Step Pyramid, near the northeast corner of its enclosure wall. Userkaf's small pyramid complex—its valley temple and causeway still as yet unexcavated—attracts attention not only by its eloquent siting near Djoser's pyramid but by reason of two particular features. First, the mortuary temple was not built at the eastern foot of the pyramid, as one would expect from the standard, religiously-motivated east–west orientation of the whole complex, but at its southern foot. The unusual sit-

Reconstruction of Userkaf's pyramid complex without causeway and valley temple (by H. Ricke).

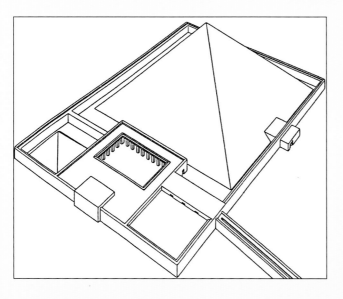

ing of the temple was almost certainly influenced by the existence of a broad and deep ditch, called the Great Moat, enclosing the precincts of Djoser's pyramid complex. The ditch ran precisely across the area where, under normal circumstances, the mortuary temple should have been sited. In order to be buried close to Djoser's pyramid, Userkaf was prepared to change the standard plan for his tomb. The second notable feature is Userkaf's wife's independent pyramid complex built to the south of the ruler's mortuary temple. The queen's mortuary temple was the largest of its kind to have been constructed up to that period.

The pyramids
of Abusir (photo:
Milan Zemina).

The majority of the Fifth Dynasty rulers had themselves buried in the cemetery at Abusir, established as an indirect result of Userkaf's construction of his sun temple here. Pyramid complexes were built at Abusir by the rulers Sahure, Neferirkare, Neferefre, and Niuserre (for further details see Chapter II). In the vicinity of their pyramids, several smaller cemeteries grew up for members of the royal families, courtiers and high state officials. It is noteworthy, however, that many of the leading dignitaries of the Fifth Dynasty did not have their tombs built at Abusir, near their kings, but at Giza or Saqqara. One example is the magnate Ti, who occupied high offices during the reigns of Neferirkare, Neferefre, and Niuserre and was even administrator of these pharaohs' pyramids and sun temples, but who built himself a tomb in North Saqqara. Ti's mastaba is considered the most beautiful of the tombs of the Old Kingdom yet discovered. This is because of the well-preserved state of its relief decorations, the artistry of their conception, the diversity of the subjects depicted from everyday life and from the mortuary cult and, last but not least, the quality of the workmanship.

Fragments of a red granite palm
column in Djedkare's pyramid
temple, south Saqqara (photo:
Milan Zemina).

Following pages:
The ruins of Unas's valley temple
at Saqqara (photo: Milan Zemina).

The tomb of Niuserre's successor Menkauhor has so far not been discovered. Some archaeologists are searching for it in North Saqqara, others in Dahshur. Menkauhor was not, however, buried at Abusir, and neither were the last two Fifth Dynasty rulers, Djedkare and Unas. Djedkare's pyramid complex, and a neighboring

Low relief with polychrome of Ptahhotep sniffing a vessel of perfumed ointment. Mastaba of Ptahhotep. Fifth Dynasty. Saqqara (photo: Milan Zemina).

Scene depicting a range of funerary offerings with boats and unfinished statues of the tomb's owner. Tomb of Irukaptah, Saqqara. Fifth Dynasty. Saqqara (photo: Milan Zemina).

and comparatively large pyramid complex of the pharaoh's wife, were built at Saqqara, roughly half way between Djoser's pyramid and the Mastabat Fara'un. The complex, already severely damaged in preceding centuries, met with misfortune of a peculiar kind in the modern period. At the end of the 1940s and beginning of the 1950s two archaeological expeditions carried out excavations there. The results of the work were not, however, made public and a part of the documentation was lost, so this complex remains one of the least-understood of all royal funerary monuments of the Old Kingdom.

The last Fifth Dynasty ruler Unas, like Userkaf, found a place for his tomb near Djoser's pyramid, but at its opposite end. Although Unas's pyramid is one of the smallest monuments of its type from the Old Kingdom, it represents a turning-point in Egyptian history. This is because on the walls

Burial chamber and sarcophagus of Unas. On the side walls of the chamber are Pyramid Texts and the ceiling is decorated to resemble a starry sky (photo: Milan Zemina).

of the pyramid's underground chambers are the first recorded religious inscriptions which Egyptologists call the Pyramid Texts. These are groups of poems, litanies, hymns, and other writings, apparently dating from various periods, but linked into a single whole, and first transcribed in the pyramid of Unas. Their purpose was to ensure the ruler a path to eternity and life among the gods in the other world. In the vicinity of Unas's mortuary temple and causeway lies a cemetery containing mastabas and rock-cut tombs, many of which belong to members of Unas's family, courtiers, high state officials, and the priests who maintained the ruler's mortuary cult. In this cemetery lies the rock-cut tomb of Nefer, with the best-preserved mummified body from the Old Kingdom, and also, among many others, what is known as the Tomb of the Two Brothers, Nyankhkhnum and Khnumhotep, a tomb which is outstandingly well-preserved and original in its relief decoration.

The pharaohs of the Sixth Dynasty built their tombs exclusively in Saqqara. The first of these, Teti, had his tomb constructed in the northern part of Saqqara near the Early Dynastic royal necropolis. His pyramid complex closely resembles that of Unas, and includes the Pyramid Texts. These texts are, in fact, to be found in all the later pyramids of the kings and even in some of the pyramids of the queens right up to the

Eighth Dynasty. Around Teti's pyramid and especially north of the monument a large cemetery was established for magnates and officials, and this contains the famous tombs of the Vizier Mereruka, the vizier Kagemni, the physician Ankhmahor, and many others. The relief decorations preserved in these tombs are astonishing for the variety of the subjects depicted, although the quality of execution often does not reach the level of the masterpieces of the Fifth Dynasty, such as those in the tomb of Ti in North Saqqara or in that of Ptahshepses at Abusir.

The pyramid complex of Pepi I is located in South Saqqara, not far from that of Djedkare. Research there, carried out by a French archaeological expedition directed by Jean Leclant and Audran Labrousse, has recently made the surprising discovery in the area around the king's pyramid of six small pyramid complexes of the wives of Pepi I. The possibility that still more remain to be discovered is not to be ruled out.

The last great pyramid complex of the Old Kingdom was built at the end of the Sixth Dynasty by Pepi II. The complex, already excavated before the Second World War by a French expedition this time led by Gustav Jéquier, lies at the southernmost edge of Saqqara, close by the Mastabat Fara'un. In layout it resembles the tombs of Pepi II's predecessors of the Sixth Dynasty. Its components also include three small pyramids and the mortuary temples of the queens Neith, Iput, and Udjebten. There is even a small cult pyramid sited near the southeastern corner of the pharaoh's pyramid. During investigation of what were hardly the most numerous remains of relief decoration in the mortuary temple it was demonstrated, surprisingly, that its creator had been inspired by the reliefs from Sahure's mortuary temple at Abusir. This is indirect proof not only of the standardization within the decoration of the royal pyramid complexes but, at the same time, also of the high artistic level of the decoration of Sahure's complex, an achievement which became the model for subsequent generations of artists and craftsmen. The same is true, in another form and at another time, of the monument of Pepi II in South Saqqara. This too later became a source of inspiration for the builders of the pyramids of the Middle Kingdom pharaohs. These, however, were for the most part not sited in the Memphite necropolis and, by the time they were built, Memphis had ceased to be the capital city of Egypt.

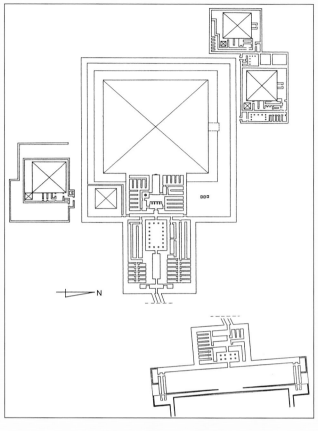

Plan of the pyramid complex of Pepi II (by G. Jéquiér).

The portrait of Ankhmahor in sunk relief. Ankhmahor's tomb. Sixth Dynasty. Saqqara (photo: Milan Zemina).

CHAPTER II

Abusir—The Rise of a Royal Necropolis

O f the sixty or so villages named Abusir in Egypt only one is an archaeological site of first-class importance; the Abusir with the cemetery of Fifth Dynasty kings. The history of Abusir is much older than the Fifth Dynasty, however.

In the Early Dynastic Period, Abusir became a rapidly growing cemetery. In south Abusir, close to the Early Dynastic cemetery in north Saqqara, a rich, upper middle class cemetery dating from the First and Second Dynasty was revealed at the beginning of the twentieth century by a German archaeological expedition directed by Hans Bonnet. Three decades later another Early Dynastic cemetery, this time belonging to the members of the lower middle class, was unearthed by the Egyptian archaeologist Rizkallah Naguib Makramallah deeper in the desert, at the mouth of Wadi Abusiri (for further details, see chapter 10). At the northern edge of Abusir, in the place called Abu Ghurab (much later, in the mid Fifth Dynasty, the king Niuserre chose the site for the construction of his sun temple), a large cemetery of the First Dynasty was found and has already been partly excavated by the Cairo University archaeological expedition led by Ali Radwan. In the Third and Fourth Dynasties especially, the middle social ranks began to build large tombs there. However, the major turning-point in the history of Abusir came at the beginning of the Fifth Dynasty. Userkaf, the first ruler of the Fifth Dynasty, selected the place as a site for the construction of the first sun temple in the Memphite necropolis. The reasons for this choice, a place approximately three kilometers north of his pyramid complex in Saqqara, have not yet come to light, and there are only conjectures about his possible motivation. Was there a royal residence or an important sun cult location

View of Sahure's pyramid from the southern portico of the pyramid temple (photo: Kamil Voděra).

in the nearby Nile Valley? Or was this, as the German Egyptologist Werner Kaiser suggested, the southernmost site from which one could see the (possibly gilded) tip of the obelisk in the temple of Re in Heliopolis? Be that as it may, the presence of Userkaf's sun temple undoubtedly became a decisive factor in the subsequent foundation of the royal cemetery in Abusir.

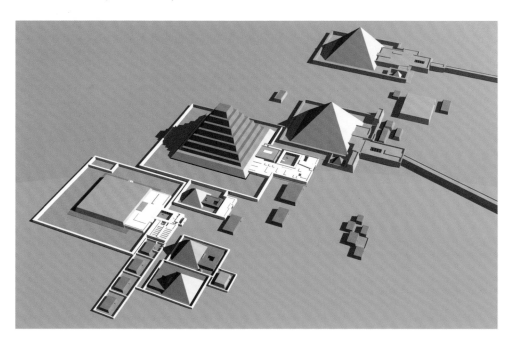

CAD reconstruction of the Abusir pyramid field (by J. Krejčí).

The first pyramid complex was built in Abusir by Sahure, who is thought likely to have been Userkaf's son. Part of the evidence for this identification is Sahure's deliberate selection of the site of his pyramid in close proximity to Userkaf's sun temple.

Perhaps because Sahure's pyramid—originally called "Sahure's-soul-shines"—resembles a small, weathered mound of rubble, early archaeologists did not pay much attention to it. Not until the beginning of the twentieth century was a fundamental investigation of the pyramid complex carried out by a German expedition, under Ludwig Borchardt's leadership. At a single stroke, his two-volume monograph, *Das Grabdenkmal des Königs Sahure* ("The Funerary Monument of the King Sahure"), a brilliant work for its time that is still frequently cited by Egyptologists, made Sahure's complex a site of great archaeological significance.

Even though Sahure's pyramid complex was not outstandingly large, it represents a turning-point in the development of royal tombs under the Old Kingdom. In comparison with the Fourth Dynasty, the volume of material used for the pyramid was reduced and there was a striking change in the layout of the mortuary temple. The reduction of the amount of stone employed, undoubtedly the result of economic considerations, was compensated for by the better quality and diversity of the types of

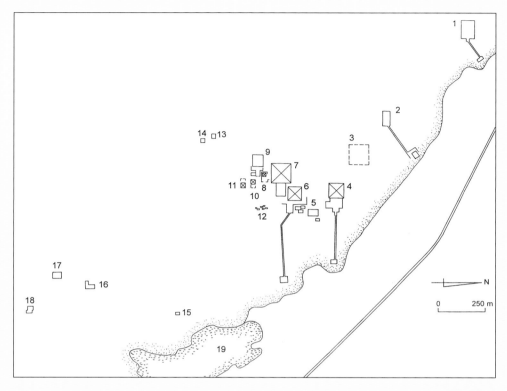

Plan of the Abusir necropolis.
1. Niuserre's sun temple;
2. Userkaf's sun temple;
3. Shepseskare's unfinished pyramid;
4. Sahure;
5. Ptahshepses mastaba;
6. Niusserre;
7. Neferirkare;
8. Khentkaus II;
9. Neferefre;
10. Lepsius no. XXIV;
11. Lepsius no. XXV;
12. Djedkare's family cemetery;
13. Udjahorresnet;
14. Jufaa;
15. Shedu;
16. Fetekti;
17. Gar, Inti;
18. Kaoper, Ity;
19. Lake of Abusir.

stone. At the same time, the relief decoration—what is called the "pictorial scheme"—of the mortuary and valley temples and the causeway is so rich in subject matter, artistic conception, and quality of workmanship that it represents the highest level of the genre that has yet been discovered from the Old Kingdom. Originally, the surface of the walls covered with these exquisite reliefs may have amounted to an unbelievable coverage of 10,000 square meters. It is therefore no wonder that Sahure's pyramid complex, its architectural plan and scheme of relief decoration, became the conceptual starting-point for the designers of the later royal tombs of the Fifth and Sixth Dynasties.

The entrance to Sahure's pyramid complex led through the valley temple which was, at the same time, a monumental gateway into the underworld residence of the deceased ruler. The temple stood at the boundary between the Nile valley and the desert at what was, for the Ancient Egyptians, the symbolic border between the World of the Living and the World of the Dead.

Sahure's valley temple has two landing ramps—one giving access from the east and one from the south. As a rule there would only be one, an eastern landing ramp, allowing access from the Nile by way of an artificial channel. Why Sahure's valley temple had two entrances has not yet been satisfactorily explained. Were there important buildings to the south? Perhaps Sahure's pyramid town—the residence of the officials, priests and artisans responsible for the construction of the complex and for

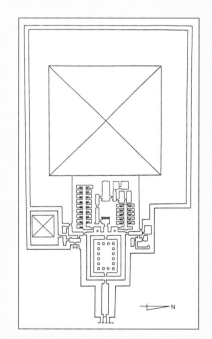

Plan of Sahure's pyramid complex (based on H. Ricke's plan with additions).

the subsequent maintenance of the mortuary cult of the pharaoh—extended in this direction. Sahure's palace *Wetjes-neferu-Sahure* "Sahure's-splendor-soars-up-to-heaven" may also have been there. Its existence is proven by inscriptions on ordinary beef fat storage jars recently found in Neferefre's mortuary temple in Abusir.

The porticoes to which each landing ramp led were decorated with pink granite columns. The walls of the porticoes and the rooms inside the temple were covered with colored pictures in low relief. Reliefs also adorned the inner walls of the causeway, i.e. the corridor which linked the valley temple to the mortuary temple. The predominant themes depicted were images of the ruler in the likeness of a sphinx treading a series of captive and bound enemies of Egypt, and others underfoot. They were apotropaia, images of a mythological character, meant to drive away approaching evil and, at the same time, to elevate the ruler's mythic godlike and sovereign role.

In 1994, Zahi Hawass decided to clean and reconstruct selected parts of Sahure's causeway. However, there was a surprising turn of events. The cleaning of the upper part of the causeway revealed huge limestone blocks decorated with iconographically and artistically unique reliefs. For reasons we can only guess, Borchardt had never investigated the sides of the upper part of the causeway. The reliefs depict, for example, the bringing of the gilded capstone for Sahure's pyramid, the celebrations and performances accompanying the conclusion of the pyramid's construction, and, most importantly, a group of impoverished Bedouins that hunger had reduced to skin and bones. The famous scene of starving, emaciated Bedouins from Unas's causeway thus lost both its uniqueness and preeminence in the repertoire of Egyptian artistic motifs. Until recently, this scene was considered unique proof of the decline of the standard of living among oasis-dwellers in the Egyptian desert that resulted from the definite ending of the wet phase in Sahara and the beginning of an arid, hot climate in the middle of the third millennium BCE. But, rather than being proof of a decline in the standard of living among the Bedouins in Sahure's or Unas's times, the scenes indicate—judging by the broader context of other scenes from Sahure's causeway— that the impoverished Bedouins might have been brought into the pyramid town to demonstrate the hardship and the dangers the pyramid builders had to contend with in bringing better qualities of stone from the remote, wild, and inaccessible mountains. No doubt, these new reliefs from Sahure's causeway shed an entirely new light on the character and significance of the pictorial scheme of the pyramid complex.

The remnants of Sahure's valley temple flooded with water (photo: Jaromír Krejčí).

In Sahure's mortuary temple we find for the first time the arrangement of rooms that was later to become the basis for the layout of temples of this type in the Old Kingdom. Access to the temple was by way of a long entrance hall in which the theme of relief decoration was the welcome to the other world given to the pharaoh by the magnates "of his time." Opening out from this entrance hall, a large open court made

Model of Sahure's valley temple (by L. Borchardt).

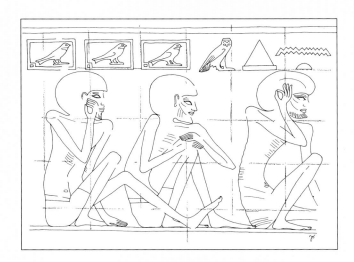

A group of squatting, emaciated Bedouins. Low relief. Sahure's causeway (by Jolana Malátková).

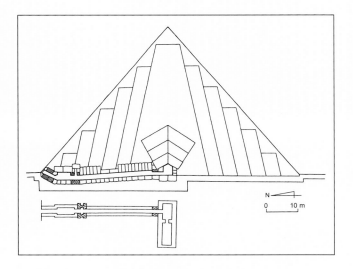

Sahure's pyramid. North–south sectional view and ground plan of the substructure (by L. Borchardt). The representation of the accretion layer-type structure of the pyramid's core is probably not correct.

up the central part of the temple. A cloister ran along its sides. The ceiling of the cloister was supported by palm columns made of pink granite and decorated with the ruler's names and symbols of the protective goddesses of Upper and Lower Egypt, the vulture Nekhbet and the cobra Wadjet. For ancient Egyptians, the palm tree was a symbol of peace, protection and affluence. According to Herbert Ricke, Sahure's courtyard thus had a special symbolic meaning, representing the sacred palm grove in Buto, the ancient Egyptians' "national cemetery." The walls of the courtyard were decorated with splendid scenes of Sahura's triumph over Asian and Libyan enemies and his magnificent spoils in colored bas-relief. Between the columns there may have originally stood statues of the pharaoh. Around the courtyard ran a corridor on whose walls also appeared beautiful scenes. They represented the ruler hunting wild desert animals. Sacrifices, including burnt offerings, would be offered up on an alabaster altar in the northwestern corner of the court.

A transverse corridor running north–south divided off the eastern, so-called public part of the temple from the western, so-called intimate part. This corridor was paved with black basalt and above the dado of red granite there again rose limestone walls covered with relief decoration of which only fragments, depicting a sea-battle and the return of trading ships from Asia, have been preserved. The intimate part of the mortuary temple included a room with five niches of red granite in which were placed statues depicting the ruler in his various sovereign forms. Until recently, opinion held that the five statues personified the five names of the king's titulary. However, this assumption was shaken by the discovery of papyri in the nearby pyramid temple of Sahure's successor, Neferirkare. The text on one of the papyri suggests that one of the statues represented the ruler as a king of Upper Egypt, a second as a king of Lower Egypt, and a third one as Osiris, the ruler of the realm of dead. The identification of the two remaining statues does not appear on the papyrus.

A passage, which only the funerary priests could use, led from the five-niche chapel to the furthermost (and in cult terms, the most important) room in the whole temple—the shadowy offering hall. On an altar in front of the huge, possibly gold plated, 'false door' through which the pharaoh's spirit could come from the other world, priests would make offerings and the prescribed rituals of the mortuary cult would be performed. Large storerooms flanking the offering hall indirectly attest to the intensity of the cult.

While excavating Sahure's mortuary temple, Borchardt found evidence of changes in the relief decoration of the mortuary temple. The figure of one of the courtiers following Sahure had been altered: not only had the symbols of royal regalia been added to his forehead, but an inscription identified the figure as that of King Neferirkare. We do not know to whom the reworked figure originally belonged. The theory that Neferirkare was Sahure's brother is based—besides other reasoning—on the assumption that the figure originally belonged to Neferirkare and that this change concerned only the upgrading of his status. Such an interpretation of similar changes to other reliefs (for example, in Haremheb's tomb), is not to be excluded although the actual circumstances could have been very different (see below concerning Shepseskare).

When complete, the pyramid which rose above the burial chamber where the mummy of Sahure rested in a basalt sarcophagus reached a height of about 48 meters. Significantly, in setting out the measurements of the pyramid, the ancient architects made a noteworthy error: the SE corner is off by about 1.58 meters to the east with respect to the NE corner, and therefore the ground plan is not entirely square.

The entrance into the pyramid's substructure is on the north wall, just above ground level. A corridor, at first descending and later slightly climbing, gives access to the antechamber, which lies directly on the pyramid's vertical axis. Both the antechamber and the burial chamber that lies further to the west were so destroyed by stone thieves that today the original plan can no longer be reconstructed with precision. The gabled ceiling consisted of three layers of enormous limestone blocks. From the royal burial, only fragments of the king's basalt sarcophagus were found. The activity of thieves in the underground parts of Sahure's pyramid—as well as other Abusir pyramids—has created a very dangerous situation. Today it is forbidden to enter the Abusir pyramids except for the unfinished pyramid of Neferefre which was so badly damaged by stone robbers in antiquity that its underground is open from above. At the end of the 1960s, the Italian researchers Vito Maragioglio and Celeste Rinaldi carried out the last measurements to be made in the underground parts of the Abusir pyramids. During the work they did not dare to speak for fear that the resonance of their voices would loosen the portions of broken ceiling blocks hanging over their heads. When necessary they exchanged directions and opinions by writing on pieces of paper.

The complex of buildings making up Sahure's tomb included yet another, miniature pyramid. It stood near the southeastern corner of the pharaoh's pyramid and had

The capital of a palm column. Sahure's pyramid temple (photo: Jaromír Krejčí).

only a cult significance. The tombs of the immediate members of Sahure's family, especially that of his wife, Neferkhanebty, and his eldest son, Netjerirenre, ought to be located to the south or southeast of the king's pyramid. These tombs, and particularly the inscriptions on their walls, could provide valuable historical evidence and answers to many questions relating to the reign of Sahure. It would, for example, be

The remnants of staircases in the store-rooms of Sahure's pyramid temple (photo: Kamil Voděra).

very interesting to know more about the fate of Sahure's first-born son, Netjerirenre, and why it was not he that inherited the throne, but Neferirkare, whose origin is still subject of conjecture.

If we estimate the length of Sahure's reign as being, at maximum, no more than fourteen years, then the reign of his successor Neferirkare was undoubtedly shorter. Probably, the latest year of rule which can so far be attributed to Neferirkare—the year of the fifth cattle count—is probably recorded on a masonry stone in the Abusir pyramid of Khentkaus II, the king's wife: Neferirkare's reign could then be considered to have lasted not more than ten years, perhaps less.

Neferirkare's pyramid—once called "Neferirkare-is-a-soul"—towers today over the whole necropolis of Abusir. It was the largest structure there, and it was also built on the highest site, 33 meters above the Nile Valley. The German scholar, Richard Lepsius, examined it briefly in the 1830s and was so fascinated by the uncovered shape of the pyramid's core that he based on it a theory that the Egyptian pyramids were constructed using inclined accretion layers. Borchardt, who thoroughly investigated the pyramid and its mortuary temple at the beginning of the twentieth century,

Opposite:
Two palm columns standing in the courtyard of Sahure's pyramid temple (photo: Kamil Voděra).

also adopted this theory. "There is perhaps no better place to study the methods used to construct the pyramids." he observed. This turned out to be a rather misleading view, as Maragioglio and Rinaldi discovered while making their measurements in the 1960s. Their conclusions, however, were not entirely precise either.

The archaeological survey carried out a few years ago by the Czech team has shown that Neferirkare's pyramid was originally conceived, and nearly completed, as a step pyramid. This is a very significant discovery, since the era of step pyramids had come to an end at the very beginning of the Fourth Dynasty, long before Neferirkare's reign. Originally, Neferirkare's pyramid had six steps, built in horizontal layers and not by the method of inclined accretion layers. Moreover, it was planned to reach a height equal to 100 Egyptian cubits, i.e. approximately 52 meters. However, its casing was not completed. When it had been cased up to roughly ten meters above the ground the decision was taken to change the stepped structure into a true pyramid. The whole construction was extended and the modified pyramid should have reached a height of about 72 meters. But this project also remained unfinished, due to the pharaoh's untimely death; only the lowest levels of the red granite blocks in which the pyramid was to have been cased were put in place.

The mortuary temple at the foot of the eastern side of the pyramid was completed by Neferirkare's successors, Neferefre and Niuserre. For reasons of economy, mud bricks and wood were used for its construction. Even the lotus columns put up inside the temple were made of wood. While the temple plan included the basic elements which, in precisely defined and mutually balanced form had already been incorporated into the royal mortuary temple scheme in Sahure's time, its overall appearance was branded by the quick and cheap execution both of the original construction and of progressive reconstruction. It is also significant that it has no causeway leading up to it. Neferirkare's sons considered it their duty to speedily complete their father's tomb and the place of his mortuary cult, i.e. the pyramid and mortuary temple, but not the causeway

North–south cross-section of Neferirkare's pyramid with a reconstruction of what are believed to have been its building phases.

and valley temple. This was despite the fact that both incomplete elements of Neferirkare's pyramid complex must, at the moment of the ruler's death, have been partially built, as is clear from the plan of the neighboring pyramid complex of Niuserre, which included a part of the foundation ramp of Neferirkare's causeway and a site originally destined for Neferirkare's valley temple.

The unfinished funerary monument of Neferirkare raises a number of questions. For instance, why did the king decide to break with earlier tradition and to return, after

View of Neferirkare's mortuary temple and pyramid from the summit of Niuserre's pyramid (photo: Kamil Voděra).

A closer view of Neferirkare's pyramid eloquently illustrates the building phases that went into the monument's construction (photo: Kamil Voděra).

A block with a fragment of a scene in low relief representing Neferirkare accompanied by his consort Khentkaus II and his eldest son Neferre.

A fragment of a clay sealing with Shepseskare's Horus name, Sekhemkhau.

about two centuries, to a tomb in the form of a step pyramid? Were the reasons connected with religion? Or were they connected with dynastic and power politics, as some previously mentioned alterations of reliefs in Sahure's mortuary temple may indicate? In the Nineteenth Dynasty king list, the famous Royal Canon of Turin, Neferirkare is considered the founder of a new dynasty. Is there a connection between this view and the original design of Neferirkare's pyramid? Did Neferirkare want to demonstrate by the stepped shape of his pyramid the beginning of a new era as Djoser had done? An unambiguous answer to these questions requires new historical sources.

The fact that Neferirkare's pyramid complex is only composed of a pyramid and a mortuary temple has had one important practical result. The funerary priests, who under normal circumstances would have lived in a so-called pyramid town in the environs of the valley temple, took up residence directly by the mortuary temple. It is probably to this unusual development that we owe the fact that the papyri of the Neferirkare temple archive have survived up to this day. Had a causeway and valley temple existed, then all written materials would probably have been archived in the administrative buildings on the edge of the Nile Valley, and today they would be buried under a layer of mud several meters deep and no trace of them would remain.

Although he was a very experienced archaeologist, during his field work in Abusir Borchardt omitted or overlooked certain things. While this did not in any way reduce the value of his discoveries and work, it is hard to understand today, for example, why he did not examine (as in the case of Sahure's causeway) the ruins of the large structure on the south side of Neferirkare's pyramid more closely. Although he made a brief exploration of it, he called off further work because he was convinced that it was a mastaba, a kind of a structure he viewed as being of secondary importance.

The Czech excavations in the late 1970s confirmed that this "mastaba" was in fact the pyramid belonging to Neferirkare's consort, Khentkaus II. At the same time, the historical context of this discovery became more complicated than it at first seemed to be. A few inscriptions on the pyramid's masonry allowed us to reach certain important conclusions. They indicated that the construction of the pyramid, originally begun for the "King's wife Khentkaus," was completed, after a lengthy interruption resulting very probably from Neferirkare's death, for the "King's mother Khentkaus." No doubt, her son thus finished the work her consort had begun. Fragments of reliefs found in a small limestone temple in front of the east side of the pyramid identify this son as Niuserre. On the only pillar found *in situ* in the temple's courtyard, Khentkaus was depicted with the uraeus on her forehead—a symbol that until this period had been reserved solely for rulers and divinities.

Still in the reign of Niuserre, Khentkaus's mortuary temple was expanded and significantly changed in both its appearance and conception. Near the southeast corner of the pyramid a small cult pyramid was built—for the first time in the pyramid complex of a queen. On the east, a group of five storerooms, a lodging for priests and a new pillared portico were added. The new perimeter wall of mud brick emphasized the importance and independence of Khentkaus II's funerary monument.

View of the pyramids of Neferefre, Khentkaus II and Lepsius nos. XXIV and XXV from the summit of Neferirkare's pyramid (photo: Kamil Voděra).

Surprisingly, the inscriptions—on relief fragments, papyri, and clay sealings—confirmed that Khentkaus II bore the same chief title as her famous namesake Khentkaus I, known from Giza from the tomb LG 100 (the so-called Fourth pyramid in Giza). An assumption that Khentkaus I and Khentkaus II were one and the same person can now safely be excluded. Most scholars interpret the title as "Mother of two kings of Upper and Lower Egypt." As in Giza, in Abusir there is clear archaeological evidence that the queen was not only buried in her tomb, but that she was long worshiped there, too. Khentkaus I, who was possibly Menkaure's daughter, lived at the end of the Fourth and the beginning of the Fifth Dynasties, whereas Khentkaus II, Neferirkare's consort and mother of Neferefre and Niuserre, lived in the middle of the Fifth Dynasty. In any event, the duplication of their titles seems to reflect the similar, and no doubt equally unusual, circumstances under which both queens lived. After the ruler's death, both of them probably had to use their authority to protect the rights of a successor to the throne who was neither first-born nor, very probably, born "to the purple." Who that was in Khentkaus I's case we do not know, but in the case of Khentkaus II it was Niuserre, whose succession to the throne, after the premature death of his elder brother Neferefre, faced obviously serious difficulties.

Following pages: View of Neferirkare's pyramid from the southwest (photo: Jaromír Krejčí).

In the 1930s, the Egyptian archaeologist Edouard Ghazouli found a block with a relief in the village of Abusir. On the stone, which very probably came from Neferirkare's mortuary temple, there is an incomplete scene depicting the king with his consort Khentkaus II and his eldest son Neferre. (This variant of the king's name is attested still from the very beginning of Neferefre's reign).

This scene, and a tiny fragment of papyrus from Neferirkare's temple archive mentioning the mortuary temple of Neferefre, were two of several reasons which led the Czech team in Abusir in the early 1980s to a hypothetical identification of the so-called Unfinished Pyramid, situated immediately SW of the pyramids of Neferirkare and Khentkaus II, with Neferefre's tomb.

In addition, the location of the Unfinished Pyramid itself offered clues for situating it chronologically. Remarkably, the pyramids of Sahure, Neferirkare, and Neferefre are arranged in the Abusir necropolis from the northeast to the southwest along a tangential line common to the northwest corner of these pyramids. The succession of the pyramids along this line thus reflects also the sequence of the kings who built these monuments. It seems that this line was a sort of axis for the Abusir pyramid field. A similar axis also existed in the necropolis at Giza. There it consisted of a line that connected the southeastern corners of the pyramids of Khufu, Khafre, and Menkaure. Both lines, that of Giza and that of Abusir, seem to cross in Heliopolis. Their point of intersection was probably in the temple of the sun god Re, at the tip of the obelisk that may thus have represented a "fixed point" in the world of the ancient Egyptians in this period.

The above-established chronological sequence of the Abusir pyramids also seems to play an important role in the solution of yet another problem.

In the oldest part of Neferefre's mortuary temple, which was not built until after the king's death, the Czech team found several sealings bearing the name Sekhemkhau, the Horus name of an almost unknown Fifth Dynasty ruler, Shepseskare, whose name is attested only in the Saqqara king list. Although in this list Shepseskare appears as the immediate predecessor of Neferefre, the archaeological context in which these sealings were found indicates that he must have been Neferefre's immediate successor instead. If Shepseskare reigned at all, then he must have done so very briefly, apparently even more briefly than Neferefre, who reigned no longer than about two years. This conclusion is indirectly corroborated by the total absence of any monuments, artifacts, or inscriptions which can be ascribed to Shepseskare, except for these few seals found in Abusir by the Czech team, two cylinders found earlier in Mit Rahina, and four other sealings revealed by Borchardt also in Abusir.

No matter how brief Shepseskare's reign was, the origin of the king can hardly be sought beyond the narrow circle of the royal family buried in Abusir. If this assumption is correct, the available historical sources indirectly indicate that he may

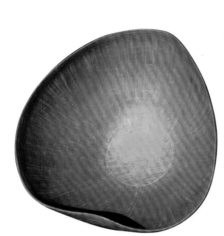

Small bowl made of fine earthenware with red coating. Early Dynastic Period. Cairo University excavations at Abu Ghurab (published by kind permission of Prof. Ali Radwan).

Following pages: A fragment of the capital of a papyrus column of red granite in Niuserre's pyramid temple (photo: Kamil Voděra).

have belonged to Sahure's rather than Neferirkare's branch of the royal family. If so, we could get closer to the explanation of a mysterious discovery made by the Czech team in Abusir.

During the early 1980s a second large unfinished pyramid was discovered in Abusir. It lies on the northern edge of the necropolis, half way between Sahure's pyramid and Userkaf's sun temple. In reality, it consists only of the traces of earthwork halted shortly after it was begun; the desert land was leveled and the excavation of the pit for the construction of the underground funerary apartment had only just commenced. It seems that the owner of this unfinished building wanted to demonstrate by his choice of the place his relationship to Sahure or Userkaf, or both. Theoretically, only two kings of the Fifth Dynasty whose pyramids had not yet been identified can be taken into consideration—Shepseskare and Menkauhor. However, according to a number of contemporaneous documents, it seems probable that Menkauhor completed a pyramid elsewhere, either in North Saqqara or Dahshur. Shepseskare, therefore, seems to be the likelier owner of the unfinished platform for a pyramid in North Abusir.

Some previously mentioned evidence appears to indicate that relations between the families of Sahure and Neferirkare might have been tense. These tensions might have affected the relationship of two kings who reigned shortly after each other, Neferefre and Shepseskare. Hypothetically, one of Sahure's sons, the surmised Shepseskare (who may not yet have been an adult at the time of his father's death) might have attempted to ascend the throne following Neferefre's untimely death. He may have taken advantage of the weakness of Neferirkare's family to launch his claim at the cost of the claim of Niuserre, the younger son of Neferirkare and Khentkaus II. Shepseskare's attempt was also doomed to disappointment, for he did not reign long and Niuserre emerged the eventual victor. The important role Khentkaus II may have played in Niuserre's ascension to the throne might explain her unusual title, the esteem in which she was held, and the additional upgrading of her mortuary cult by Niuserre.

Niuserre's pyramid complex, excavated at the beginning of the twentieth century by Borchardt, is unusual in many respects. Even its siting is curious. Had the previously described basic axis of the Abusir cemetery been respected, Niuserre's pyramid would have had to be built to the southwest of Neferefre's. This, however, would have meant a site deep in the desert and more than a kilometer away from the edge of the Nile Valley. The costs of construction would have been too high. Moreover,

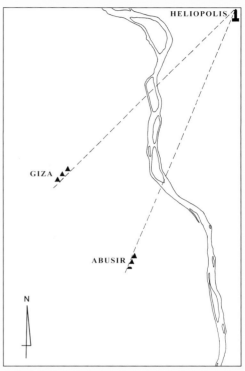

The axes of the necropolises in Giza and Abusir were probably directed toward Heliopolis.

we should not forget that on his ascent to the throne Niuserre took on the obligation of completing the three half-built pyramid complexes of his predecessors and the nearest members of his family (his father Neferirkare, his mother Khentkaus II and his elder brother Neferefre). The pharaoh therefore decided to use the modest free space close to his father's tomb and to build his pyramid and mortuary temple near the northeastern corner of Neferirkare's pyramid. For two small pyramid complexes, thought to be the tombs of Niuserre's and Neferefre's (?) consorts, known as Lepsius XXIV and Lepsius XXV, there was no place next to the king's pyramid. These two monuments had to be built at the very southern edge of the Abusir pyramid field.

The site for Niuserre's valley temple and parts of the causeway he took over from the building project for the tomb of his father. This decision, which was certainly not an usurpation but rather an act of filial piety, significantly influenced the building project. Moreover, the plan also had to respect a small group of mastabas that had already been built in the time of Sahure and Neferirkare to the east of the site of the future pyramid of Niuserre. All these topographical and archaeological factors were reflected in the layout of the mortuary temple, and this is why the overall plan of Niuserre's pyramid complex, which bears the poetic name, "Enduring-are-the-cult-places-of-Niuserre," is atypical. If the basic outline of the standard mortuary temple of the Fifth or Sixth Dynasty resembles the letter "T," then Niuserre's mortuary temple can be said to bear more resemblance to the letter "L." But despite this modification of basic layout, the temple contains all the fundamental elements already established as the norm for this kind of building in the reign of Sahure.

However, some interesting new features also appeared within this structure. One of these was a small room on the

boundary between the public and intimate parts of the temple. In this room was placed a large red granite statue of a lion (today in the Egyptian museum in Cairo), the symbolic guardian of the pharaoh's privacy in the underworld. The second was a small rectangular room between the five niches and the offering hall, which from this time on became a permanent element of the layout of mortuary temples and for which Egyptologists have come to use the term *antichambre carrée* or "square room." The walls of the temple rooms were originally richly decorated in low relief, not differing greatly in subject matter or quality from those of Sahure's mortuary temple.

In Niuserre's mortuary temple we meet with yet another innovation which was later to have a marked influence on the appearance of Ancient Egyptian architecture. High tower-shaped buildings with slightly sloping outer walls were erected at the northeast and southeast corners of the temple. At the top these terminated in flat terraces, accessible by staircase. In these gigantic corner buildings we can possibly see the prototype of pylons, the monumental gates of later Ancient Egyptian temples and palaces.

In addition to Niuserre's pyramid, two small pyramid complexes were built during the king's reign, as indicated by some mason's marks and the horizontal stratigraphy of the site. Judging by their plan, they belonged to queens. Both small complexes, each consisting of a pyramid and a mortuary temple, were built south of the

Basin for waste water. Reddish quartzite. Niuserre's pyramid temple (photo: Kamil Voděra).

Opposite:
A fragment of Khekeretnebty's mummy wrapping. On the linen wrapping is a cursive inscription containing the name and titles of the overseer of the workshop in which the linen was produced (photo: Milan Zemina).

pyramid complex of Khentkaus II. From both complexes, only scanty remains have survived and since there is no clear-cut evidence concerning the identity of their owners, they are called after Lepsius's archaeological map "pyramid no. XXIV" and "pyramid no. XXV." In the badly damaged burial chamber of pyramid no. 24 fragments of the royal sarcophagus in red granite, the remnants of the burial equipment and, most importantly, the mummy of woman aged between 20 to 24 years, probably a spouse of either Niuserre or Neferefre were discovered. Regarding pyramid no. 25, the archaeological examination of the monument is just beginning at the time of writing.

A wooden base with the remnants of feet is all that remains of a striding statue of the director of the palace, Mernefu (photo: Milan Zemina).

Statue of Princess Hedjetnub shortly after it was discovered. Wood with remains of stucco and polychrome (photo: Jan Brodský).

Not far from pyramid no. 24, at the eastern outskirts of the Abusir pyramid field, a small cemetery with mastabas of less important members of Djedkare's family was discovered. It still remains rather enigmatic why these people—princesses Khekeretnebty and Hedjetnub, prince Neserkauhor, and others—were buried at Abusir and why they were not buried near Djedkare's pyramid in South Saqqara. Small though the cemetery is, this burial site is of particular interest because it combines the burials of a relatively large number of women as well as the concentrated burials of some of King Djedkare's family. What is also interesting is that these royal children were buried together with their tutor, Idu.

After the death of Niuserre everything changed in the Abusir necropolis. His successors abandoned Abusir and built their monuments in other places. After a period of about sixty years, Abusir ceased to be the royal cemetery. However, private tombs continued to be built, especially in South Abusir. The cults in the Abusir pyramid temples continued for perhaps one and half century more, through the end of the Old Kingdom. Shortly afterwards, the Abusir pyramids were robbed. The renewed but substantially restricted mortuary cults at the Abusir pyramid temples at the beginning of the Middle Kingdom survived, however, for only a short period and then died out forever. After this Abusir fell into complete oblivion for more than half a millennium. People returned there at the beginning of the New Kingdom when the cult of Sakhmet—possibly stimulated by the relief of the lion goddess which once adorned the corridor around the open columned courtyard—developed in the ruins of Sahure's pyramid temple. Interestingly, it was on exactly the same spot that a small Coptic shrine appeared much later. But these succeeding chapters in the history of the Abusir necropolis, no matter how intriguing and important, were no longer directly linked to the Egyptian pharaohs.

CHAPTER III

Under the Sign of the Sun

From ancient times man's spirit has been drawn towards the sun, that mysterious radiant heavenly body which brings both benefit and destruction, life and death. Yet rarely has fascination with the sun reached the level that it did in Ancient Egypt. Undoubtedly a factor contributing to this was the particular natural environment of Egypt, a fertile strip of land stretching along the banks of the Nile from south to north and closed in on both sides to east and west by seemingly unending and eternally scorched desert. The fertile valley and the desert, water and sun—so sharp yet so imperceptible a border between prosperity and wretchedness, good and evil, life and death. Here terror and measureless respect flowed together in man into a feeling of absolute dependence on the sun, ruler of the world.

We can only guess at the beginnings of sun worship in the Nile Valley. Undoubtedly they reach back far into prehistory. The earliest direct evidence is to be found with the first development of Egyptian writing at the dawn of Egypt's historic era. The oldest hieroglyphic writing already shows the sun denoted by the simple yet very realistic sign of a disc. This pictorial semantic sign, an ideogram, could also be transcribed by means of phonograms and then sounded as *re* (the vowel "e" is not transcribed with complete precision since it refers to a guttural sound resembling our "e," "a," and "o" all at once). Philologists suggest that its meaning is possibly connected with the Egyptian word *ier* which meant "to rise," or "to come forth." The etymology of the word *re* has not, however, been satisfactorily identified. The beginnings of the deification of the sun and the development of its cult are also obscure. It appears that in the earliest times the cult of the sun was popular mainly among peo-

Saqqara necropolis
in a sandstorm
(photo Milan Zemina).

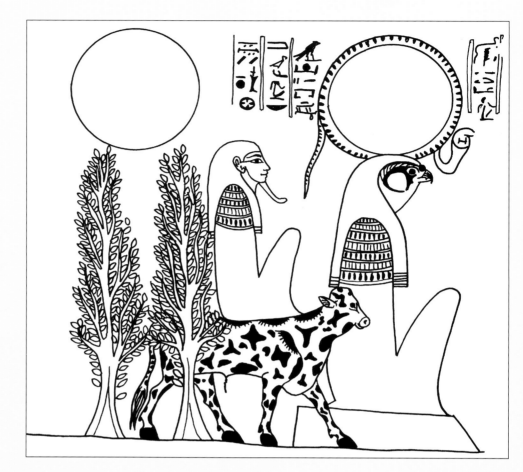

Falcon-headed
Re-Harakhty and
Atum seated on a
calf represent two
manifestations of
the sun god Re.
Wall painting.
Senedjemib's tomb
in Deir al-Medina.
Nineteenth Dynasty
(by J. Malátková).

ple of the lowest social strata and that in the second half of the fourth millennium
BCE the sun god Re was overshadowed by other, more significant, deities. If we leave
to one side the rather debatable evidence for the theo-form character of the names of
two second Dynasty rulers, Nebre and Neferkare, in which the word *re* is an element,
then it seems that the real, one might almost say unstoppable, advance of the sun god
and his cult began from the Third Dynasty with the reign of Djoser, who was the
founder of the strictly centralized state known in the periodisation of Egyptian history as the Old Kingdom (approximately from the 28th to the 22nd century BCE).

The sun god Re was pictured as a man with the sun disc on his head. Later he
acquired other attributes and could be depicted in other forms such as a sitting cat or
man with the head of a cat. Gradually Re became not merely the object of a cult but
the subject of complex theological speculations and the highest deity of Ancient
Egypt. The basic ideology of the Ancient Egyptian state consisted of the idea that
Egypt was the work of the gods, an island of order and justice surrounded by an end-
less sea of chaos. The Egyptian ruler, the Pharaoh, the only god to live among men
on earth, was the guarantee that hostile forces of internal and external evil would not
prevail over the forces of order and good. Order, truth, and justice were embodied by

Re's daughter *Maat*, pictured as a seated woman with an ostrich feather in her hair. The ostrich feather, having the same sound value *maat*, became the symbol of the goddess and, together with her, of order, truth, and justice. In theological constructions Re emerges as a universal cosmic deity, the creator, ruler of the gods, god of the dead, and ruler of the other world. He played an important role in myth and magic. According to an ancient myth the sun god was born each morning from the sky goddess Nut on the eastern horizon in the form of the god Khepre. Here he began his daily journey across the heavenly ocean in a barge called *mendjet* so that in the evening on the western horizon he could descend as the god Atum. At night his journey continued in the night sky through the underworld in a barge called *mesketet*. And so on and on, continuously from the creation of the world until its end.

The god Re in the shape of a tomcat killing the snake Apophis. Wall painting. Inherkhau's tomb, Deir al-Medina. Nineteenth Dynasty (photo: Milan Zemina).

In various representations of his aspects, or in combination with other gods, Re was worshipped in many places in Egypt. The oldest, and in the Old Kingdom also the most important, center of the cult of Re was *Iunu*, later called Heliopolis, "the solar city" in Greek. This lay on the eastern margins of modern Cairo. Here the best known and largest temples of Re were built, including what was known as "The High Sand," a structure which gave material form to the mythical hill which at the creation of the world first emerged from the primeval waters and on which the radiance of the sun first shone. In the sacred places of the temple, called the "House of Benben," worship was offered to the *benben*, an ancient stone fetish perhaps in the shape of a cone or a pyramid symbolizing the summit on which the sun was born daily. The shape of this particular fetish is usually linked to the original form of the royal tombs of the Old Kingdom—the pyramid. The priests of Re from Heliopolis, and in particular Re's High Priest, who in the earliest period was called "Through whom the Highest is Gazed upon," and later the "One who sees the Great One [the God]" or "The Greatest of Seers," gained ever greater importance and influence. Another significant center of the cult of Re was the Ancient Egyptian *Sakhebu*, a place not as yet precisely located but probably lying on the west bank of the Nile opposite Heliopolis and near modern Zat al-Kom. Both of these places played an important part both in the obscure period of the fall of the Fourth Dynasty and rise of the Fifth Dynasty and in the establishment and development of the royal cemetery at Abusir. Abusir was, after all, chosen as their final resting-place by the Fifth Dynasty pharaohs, who were sometimes termed "Solar Kings." Several of these kings also built what are known as sun temples here.

The English traveler and collector of antiquities Henry Westcar, during his stay in Egypt in the mid-nineteenth century, acquired a papyrus which to this day bears his name and represents a highly significant Ancient Egyptian literary source. On the papyrus, which dates from the Hyksos Period, four stories have been preserved which are in fact only a fragment and copy of an apparently older and longer text. The first story among these tales is set in the time of the Fourth Dynasty and takes place at the court of the famous Pharaoh Khufu. It describes how the sons of the Pharaoh came into his presence and related the remarkable things that had occurred in the reigns of his predecessors Nebka and Sneferu. The account also mentions the magician Djedi. The hundred and ten year-old Djedi was summoned and asked to demonstrate his arts to the Pharaoh. During one of the wonders which he performed Djedi predicted the miraculous birth of three kings—founders of a new dynasty. He was thus indirectly informing the Pharaoh of the extinction of his line. The alarm that seized the Pharaoh was such that Djedi could then do no more than comfort him with the words: "Your son, his son, (and only then) one of them." Another two generations of the line of Khufu were to follow each other on the throne of the pharaohs. According to the prophecy of Djedi, the new rulers—Userkaf, Sahure, and Neferirkare—would be born through the supernatural union of the sun god Re himself and an ordinary woman named Rudjdjedet, the wife of a priest of Ra from Sakhebu.

Egyptologists have taken up the designation of "Solar Kings" for the new rulers who founded the Fifth Dynasty. It seems that beneath the apparently innocent fairy-tale of the Westcar Papyrus there lies a hidden political and propaganda purpose. This was perhaps to give additional explanation for and justify the changes in the leadership of the state and the rise of a new dynasty. To speak of a "new dynasty" is not perhaps quite accurate and it might be more appropriate to speak of a partial violation of the strict rules governing succession to the throne that served the interests of a collateral branch of the royal family. The prophecy of Djedi was not entirely accurate, since after the death of Khufu three successors who were demonstrably his heirs followed him on the throne—his two sons Radjedef and Khafre and his grandson Menkaure, in that order. Only after the death of Menkaure did the reign of the Fourth Dynasty meet its so far still obscure end. For other reasons as well the story from the Westcar Papyrus cannot be regarded as a direct historical source but only as a later literary reflection on historical events that probably originated at the end of the Fourth Dynasty and beginning of the Fifth Dynasty (for more of the story of this Papyrus see Chapter IV).

Obscurity also surrounds the reasons that led the first pharaohs of the Fifth Dynasty to found the new royal necropolis in Abusir, at the time a by no means outstandingly significant place between Saqqara and Giza. Some Egyptologists believe that Abusir was chosen because an important place of the sun cult might have existed somewhere nearby in the Nile valley. Others see the special significance of Abusir in the fact that it was the southernmost spot from which it was still possible to glimpse the sun shining on the top of the obelisk of Re's temple in Heliopolis.

The first to start building in Abusir was Userkaf, the founder of the Fifth Dynasty and a man of uncertain origin, possibly a collateral son of the royal family, maybe a High Priest of Re from Heliopolis, or even both. Userkaf provided the impetus for the establishment of the royal necropolis in Abusir, even if he had his own tomb built in Saqqara near the northeastern corner of Djoser's pyramid complex. This is because he built the first sun temple in Abusir. In this way he opened the brief and still in many ways mysterious and obscure chapter of Egyptian history that is represented by the sun temples built in the Memphite necropolis.

"Re's Stronghold" (or perhaps "Re's storage house") was the name given to Userkaf's sun temple. Its ruins are to be found today on a hill north of Sahure's pyramid in Abusir. The name of the temple is taken from Nekhen, a stronghold in Upper Egypt and the seat of the earliest, still prehistoric, kings whose achievements led progressively to the victorious conclusion of the efforts to unite Egypt. Did Userkaf, in using this name, want to give symbolic expression to the final victory in the struggle to assert the cult of Re and the invincibility of the stronghold of the new faith?

The building in some respects resembles a pyramid complex. It consists of a valley temple on the edge of the desert, a causeway, and a temple erected on a hill, roughly

Following pages:
The ruins of Userkaf's sun temple. In the background the Abusir pyramids are visible (photo: Kamil Voděra).

20 meters high, above the Nile Valley. Here, of course, the likeness ends. The design of the complex of buildings making up the sun temple differs completely in both overall conception and detailed execution from the contemporary royal tomb in the form of a pyramid. Above all, there is the strikingly different orientation of the sun temple complex. Only the "upper" temple with the obelisk is precisely oriented in an east–west direction. The other elements in the complex—the valley temple and the causeway leading to the temple with the obelisk—were not oriented by the cardinal points. This fact is particularly surprising in the case of the valley temple. This building on the edge of the Nile Valley was not, after all, simply a monumental "gate" to the whole complex but a genuine temple, albeit one atypical in its layout. It was rectangular in shape and was made up of an antechamber, middle section with an open court with pillars, and, finally, of seven niches in the rear section. In Ancient Egypt precise orientation to the cardinal points was an integral part of the rituals accompanying the establishment of a temple, whether the axis of the temple was east–west or north–south. The peculiarities of the valley temple in

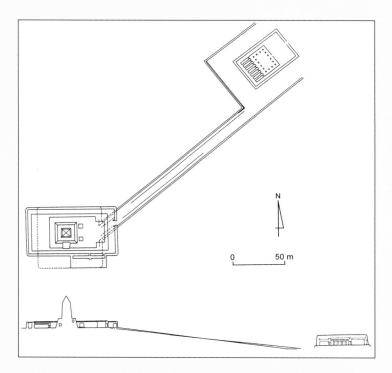

Horizontal plan and lengthwise cross-section of the building complex of Userkaf's sun temple (by H. Ricke).

question led Herbert Ricke and his colleagues on the joint Swiss-German archaeological expedition that excavated the Userkaf sun temple complex in the mid-1950s to the theory that it was older than the rest of the complex into which it had been incorporated. They even considered the possibility that it had originally been a sanctuary of the goddess Neith, an idea based on the discovery of the head of a statue made of black slate with a partially preserved Lower Egyptian crown. By chance this statue fragment was found only a few hours before the completion of excavations in the precincts of Userkaf's sun temple. Ultimately, however, the theory was rejected because more detailed analysis showed that there were traces of a black moustache painted under the nose. It was therefore concluded that it was not a portrait of the goddess Neith, but of the pharaoh Userkaf himself (the statue is now exhibited in the Egyptian Museum in Cairo). This explanation does not, of course, answer the basic question of the unusual layout and orientation of the valley temple of Userkaf's complex at Abusir.

The causeway, a sort of open ramp that linked the valley temple to the temple with the obelisk which was located on higher ground, is also unusual in position and orientation. The causeway does not lie along the main axis of either of the two temples. It is a pity that we are unable to compare the causeway of Userkaf's sun temple complex with that of his pyramid complex in Saqqara. This is because neither the valley temple nor the causeway of the latter complex has been excavated yet. The position of Userkaf's causeway in Abusir does, however, indicate that its architects to a certain extent drew inspiration from the tomb complexes of Userkaf's predecessors Menkaure in Giza and Shepseskaf in south Saqqara.

The most significant part of Userkaf's complex in Abusir was the temple with the obelisk. The temple gradually underwent extensive reconstruction, which markedly changed its appearance. Originally, it had a square ground plan, but it was then extended and the ground plan was modified to a rectangular design, oriented east–west. The greater part of the temple, roughly its eastern half, was filled by a large open court. In the western half there was a large, stone obelisk, the symbol of the sun cult. Archaeological research into its construction, however, has resulted in the very surprising discovery that the obelisk was not a part of the original temple but was erected as a later addition. Originally a low building resembling a mastaba in shape had stood there, possibly supporting a wooden column with an image of the sun disc. Here, evidently, there was once an altar accessible by a low staircase. After the reconstruction, the altar, on which offerings were made, was positioned in front of the eastern side of the base of the huge obelisk. From written sources we know that the obelisk was of red granite and that it was the ruler Neferirkare who caused it to be erected in Userkaf's temple. On two sides of the altar, to the north and south, shrines of diorite were built in which there probably stood statues of Re and Hathor, the deities venerated in the sun temple. The temple also included magazines. It was surrounded by a huge enclosure wall with rounded

Head of colossal red granite statue of Userkaf. Egyptian Museum (JE 52501), Cairo (photo: Milan Zemina).

Niuserre's sun temple at Abu Ghurab. The pyramids at Giza can be seen in the background (photo: Milan Zemina).

Alabaster tubs from the so-called Great Slaughterhouse of Niuserre's sun temple at Abu Ghurab (photo: Kamil Voděra).

outer corners. It is not yet established whether this rounded effect had a merely constructional-functional significance, for example to provide greater resistance to damage, or perhaps also a religious meaning, for example to resemble the Primeval Hill on which the sun had shone at the creation of the world.

Only a few hundred meters to the north of the Userkaf sun temple, at a place called Abu Ghurab (which translated from the Arabic means "Father of Ravens") lie the ruins of the second sun temple to have been found and investigated archaeologically so far—that of Niuserre. Excavations were carried out here as early as the end of the last century by the German archaeological expedition led by Friedrich Wilhelm von Bissing. The member of the expedition entrusted with the task of documenting and processing the architectonic discoveries was Ludwig Borchardt, the architect and archaeologist who was later to contribute significantly to archaeological investigation of the neighboring pyramid cemetery in Abusir.

Niuserre's sun temple bore the very exalted name "Delight of Re." Again, it was composed of three parts: a valley temple, a causeway, and a temple with an obelisk. This temple too was not precisely aligned to the cardinal points. Here, however, as had not been the case with Userkaf's complex, the von Bissing expedition was able to uncover the surroundings of the valley temple. As excavations proceeded, it was shown that the huge stone enclosure wall of a town, which had apparently extended far towards the east in the Nile Valley, abutted on the valley temple. Of course, the existence of this town—whether contemporary with or older than Niuserre's complex, does not explain the disharmony in the orientation of the valley temple to the cardinal points. Niuserre's valley temple was simpler than neighboring Userkaf's in layout. It might be more appropriate to speak of it as a matter of a monumental gateway to Niuserre's complex than as a valley temple. A huge structure made of limestone blocks, it had columned porticos on three sides: a main entrance approached from the east and decorated with four palm columns of red granite, and side entrances on the northwest and southeast each decorated with only one pair of these columns. The gateway allowed access to the open causeway, which was built in technically demanding conditions: a 16 meter vertical difference had to be overcome over a relatively short distance and also over very uneven ground. Limestone blocks were also the material used for construction of the causeway.

The hill on which Niuserre's temple with the obelisk stood was comparatively small. Before construction of the temple, it was necessary to extend the summit with a system of artificial terraces. The temple has a rectangular layout with an east–west orientation defined by a huge periphery wall built of limestone blocks. Roughly the southeastern quarter of the temple was taken up by a large open court. The northeastern quarter consisted of a series of storage chambers and an open space, which

Borchardt called the Great Slaughterhouse. This was because here he discovered several large alabaster basins—circular bowls carved out of a roughly cubed block—which were positioned in cascading order one after the other so that the blood of the sacrificial beasts could flow freely down them. The limestone paving of the slaughterhouse was provided with grooves, which would, at the same time, facilitate the run-off of liquid. In his reconstruction of the original layout Borchardt postulated the existence of a second similar but smaller slaughterhouse in the northwestern corner of the temple. However, Borchardt's interpretation of both the spaces mentioned as slaughterhouses has one serious weakness. Neither in the Great nor Small "Slaughterhouse," nor anywhere else in the whole temple, has any unmistakable archaeological evidence of the killing of sacrificial animals been found. In particular, there has been no sign of the characteristic conical stone blocks, which have a hole and which were anchored in the ground, to which the prone and bound beasts were tied before slaughter. Such blocks, with their eloquent archaeological testimony, have been found in the "Sanctuary of the Knife" in the precincts of the Neferefre pyramid complex in Abusir. Niuserre's temple has also yielded no other kinds of evidence characteristic of slaughterhouses, such as animal bones, flint knives, etc. It appears that rather than being used for the slaughter of animals these spaces were employed for the ritual purification of the offerings, including meat, to be laid on the altar of the sun god.

The altar stood in the open courtyard almost at the center of the temple. It was made of five enormous alabaster blocks with the central block having an upper surface circular in form (symbolizing a rounded offering table or, as the case may be, a stylized hieroglyphic sign *re*) and the four lateral blocks, facing the cardinal points, having surfaces carved in the form of the hieroglyphic symbol *hetep*, which means "offering" or "offering table." Intriguingly, in the shape of the blocks of the altar, the name *hetep re* "Re's offering table" was encoded. And that is the name of Neferfre's sun temple (for further details, see the text below). The altar, which has remained to this day in a relatively good state of preservation, represents the most beautiful example of its type not only from the Old Kingdom, but from Ancient Egypt in its entire history.

The altar stood at the eastern foot of an immense stone pedestal, 20 meters high, from which a 36-meter obelisk soared toward the sky. The pedestal was in the form of a truncated pyramid. It was built of limestone blocks and its outer walls were faced with red granite blocks. A corridor led through it, slanting upward to allow access to the top of the pedestal at the foot of the obelisk. The corridor walls were decorated with exquisite scenes in low relief, of which, alas, only a part has survived. Among these were found the unique pictures known as the "Seasons" which depict the changing natural background during the Ancient Egyptian seasons of inundation and harvest. The scenes from the third part of the year, the season of emergence (of the fields from the flood or of the crops from the ground), have not survived. The von Bissing expedition removed the reliefs and took them to Germany where today they are one of the most valuable of the exhibits in the Egyptian Museum in Berlin (*die Weltkammer*, or the Chamber of Seasons). In the ruins of the pedestal the German expedition also found fragments of scenes of the festival of *sed*, an important religious ceremony in which the ruler would celebrate the jubilee of his ascent to the throne and at the same time would be reconfirmed in his office. Only fragments of the

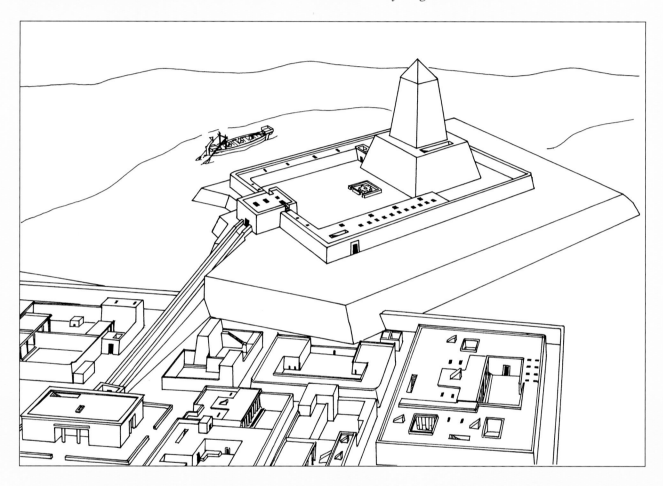

Reconstruction of Niuserre's sun temple at Abu Ghurab (by L. Borchardt).

obelisk, which once towered to a height of 36 meters, have survived. It was not made from one piece of stone but from limestone blocks. This facilitated its later destruction when the temple became an easily accessible quarry.

Outside the temple and near its southern side, the German expedition discovered a large building resembling a boat. It was built of mud bricks, plastered, whitewashed and colored and augmented with several other elements made of other materials, for example wood. It had a purely symbolic character and it is believed to have been a representation of the so-called 'solar boat' in which, according to the Ancient Egyptian conception, the sun god was supposed to float across the heavenly ocean.

Fragment of a relief with scenes of sealing vessels containing honey, mating sheep and catching birds. Chamber of Seasons, Niuserre's sun temple at Abu Ghurab (by E. Edel and S. Wenig).

The sun temples of Userkaf and Niuserre are the only two monuments of their kind yet to have been discovered and archaeologically investigated. Contemporary written sources, however, and especially inscriptions in the tombs of magnates and high officials from the Fifth Dynasty, as well as papyri from the archives of the Abusir pyramid complexes, mention six sun temples. The temples were built only by rulers of the Fifth Dynasty, though not all of them. Apart from Userkaf and Niuserre, a sun temple was built—or, at least, the construction of such a temple was begun—by Sahure, Neferirkare, Neferefre, and Menkauhor. It is needless to emphasize that the quest for these four—as yet undiscovered—temples has become one of the great challenges for future generations of archaeologists in Egypt.

Sahure's sun temple, "Field of Re," is mentioned very rarely in the contemporaneous sources and, when it is, it is always with the determinative of a pedestal without an obelisk, from which it can be inferred that its construction remained unfinished. This is surprising, especially as Sahure founded it, according to the annals of the Palermo Stone, shortly after he ascended the throne and provided it with fields and offerings. A few limestone blocks bearing the name of the temple have, however, been discovered in the masonry of Niuserre's mortuary temple (the so-called Northern *Eckbau*, a massive, tower-like structure in the northeast corner of the temple) in Abusir. Perhaps these were blocks which were left over after the completion of Sahure's temple, or perhaps Sahure's sun temple was never completed and the material prepared for it was used for other purposes. Werner Kaiser gave voice to the assumption that Sahure's sun temple stood in the place of Niuserre's pyramid and existed there for only a brief period of time. If the core of Kaiser's theory is correct, a very puzzling discovery made in the mid-1970s by the Czech team near the northeast corner of Niuserre's pyramid temple would open the way to an exciting archaeological conclusion.

During the Czech excavations in the area around the southwest corner of the mastaba of Ptahshepses (see Chap. VII), and very close to the Northern *Eckbau*, numerous fragments of a large red granite obelisk, including the pyramidion, perhaps once gilded with copper sheets, were found. It is certain that the obelisk (originally at least ten meters high) had never been part of the mastaba of Ptahshepses. Very probably, the obelisk stood on a stone platform, the remnants of which were found by Borchardt next to the Northern *Eckbau*. The possibility cannot therefore be ignored *a priori* that Kaiser's hypothesis is right and that Sahure might have begun the construction of his sun temple on the top of the hillock on which Niuserre's pyramid now stands. The temple might have remained unfinished because Sahure preferred to

complete his pyramid complex first. Niuserre could have later decided to build his pyramid complex at the same place, and to dismantle the unfinished monument and reuse its elements in his own construction.

Whatever the answer, Sahure's sun temple apparently did not stand far from Abusir. Archaeologists are also still looking for the "Place of Re's Pleasure," the sun temple of Neferirkare. This was probably the largest of the sun temples built under the Fifth Dynasty, and, in any case, the one most frequently mentioned in contemporary inscriptions. Concerning Neferirkare's sun temple, one has the impression that this monument, though provided with an obelisk (as attested by all contemporaneous written evidence), was a more modest building than that of Niuserre in Abu Ghurab and, possibly, even that of Userkaf in north Abusir. It cannot be excluded that this temple was mostly built in mud brick and could have later been largely

A scene of the sed festival, preserved on a fragment of low relief from Niuserre's sun temple in Abu Ghurab. It shows the ruler, wearing the crown of Upper Egypt and a tight fitting mantel, in various episodes of the festival (by F. v. Bissing).

destroyed by *sabbakhin* ("fertilizer men" who search for decayed ancient mudbrick masonry to use it as a fertilizer for their fields), which might be another reason why the search for this lost monument has been futile to date.

Quite recently, the German archaeologist Rainer Stadelmann proposed identifying the as yet undiscovered sun temples of Sahure and Neferirkare with Userkaf's sun temple. This theory, according to which Userkaf's sun temple was successively completed and, at the same time, appropriated for their personal use by Sahure and Neferirkare, is not very convincing. Among masons' inscriptions found within Userkaf's ruined temple, not a single fragment of the name of either Sahure's sun temple or Neferirkare's sun temple was found. Moreover, this theory does not seem to agree with the evidence of the papyri from Neferirkare's mortuary temple. As a matter of fact, some offerings (for example, pieces of meat) were transported to the latter temple by means of a boat in the time of Djedkare. The use of a boat to traverse the short distance between Userkaf's sun temple and Neferirkare's mortuary temple does not seem to be very likely: it was only about 500 meters across the desert. Why would the servants take a boat to make the journey?

Neferefre's sun temple, called "Re's Offering Table," has also so far proved impossible to find. This is perhaps not so surprising, since this ruler reigned for too short a time for his sun temple to have been completed. Either this temple, mentioned only once in inscriptions from the famous tomb of the magnate Ti in Saqqara, was abandoned shortly after building had commenced, or the site was used by one of Neferefre's successors. In this connection, research on the remains of the huge brick structures which the von Bissing expedition found under the ruins of Niuserre's sun temple at Abu Ghurab is interesting and certainly worth more thorough archaeological investigation. As a matter of fact, these structures seem to be more than the mere remnants of supply ramps and auxiliary buildings preceding the erection of the temple. One can hardly resist the temptation to see a deeper symbolical meaning in the shape of the blocks of the alabaster altar in Niuserre's sun temple, namely the possibility that it represented the encoded name of Neferefre's sun temple *Hetep-re* "Re's offering table." If so, did Niuserre complete Neferefre's unfinished sun temple for himself and, as an act of piety to his deceased brother, let the name of the original temple be encoded in the shape of the altar?

The last sun temple, built by the little-known pharaoh Menkauhor, and named "Horizon of Re" or "The Place where Re Issues Forth," has likewise still not been found. Judging by rare evidence of this monument in contemporaneous inscriptions, it too was probably never finished. The last rulers of the Fifth Dynasty, Djedkare, and Unas, on the other hand, gave up the construction of sun temples entirely.

The reasons which lay behind the building of sun temples at the beginning of the

Jean-Phillip Lauer
by the red granite
pyramidion of an
obelisk discovered in
April 1974 near the
southwestern corner
of the mastaba of
Ptahshepses (photo:
Milan Zemina).

Fifth Dynasty and the reasons why such building ceased towards the end of the dynasty have not yet been satisfactorily explained. Undoubtedly the task has been made difficult by the fact that, of six sun temples, it has so far proved possible to locate and archaeologically investigate only two. Information is incomplete and there exist only a series of more or less plausible suppositions. It is clear from the names and design of the two temples so far investigated that these temples were closely connected with the worship of the sun (more precisely, with the setting, or dying, sun) and that the central cult object was an obelisk, the solar symbol *par excellence*. The fact that the temples—both those already located and very probably the others as well—were built on the west bank of the Nile, in places where the sun set, and in the middle of the Memphite necropolis nevertheless shows that they were also linked to conceptions of the after-life and above all to the royal mortuary cult. This is, in any case, amply confirmed by the information provided by papyri from the Abusir temple archives. From these we know that it was from the sun temples that many of the sacrifices—especially meat, vegetables, etc.—would come to the royal mortuary temples. The offerings would first be placed on the altar of Re in a sun temple and only then distributed to serve the needs of royal mortuary cults. It is interesting that a sun temple would not only supply the mortuary temple of the ruler who had built it, but would supply those of other pharaohs as well. The sun temple would then not only have been the place of the setting sun, the "mortuary temple of the sun" but, in both religious and economic terms, an integral part of the building complex of a ruler's tomb and his mortuary cult. It also appears that the short history of sun temples was closely linked with the destiny of the royal cemetery in Abusir. This was because the sun temples were built above all by the rulers buried in Abusir. Moreover, two out of the six sun temples have already been found in the immediate neighborhood of Abusir.

Just as the foundation of the royal cemetery in Abusir was evidently influenced by Userkaf's decision to build the first of the sun temples in that place, so the abandonment of the Abusir cemetery by Djedkare was probably one reason why sun temples ceased to be built. There must, nonetheless, have been still more weighty reasons. Was one of these Djedkare's fundamental reorganization of the royal mortuary cults at the Abusir cemetery (for a detailed account see below, Chapter VI)? Was one factor the political and administrative interests that lay behind the pharaoh's transfer of not only the royal cemetery but also the royal residence to another place—to what today is South Saqqara? Or, were the decisive reasons religious and linked to the "popularization" of the burial cult and the rise of the worship of Osiris which occurred just at the time of Djedkare ? There are many unanswered questions but the greatest of them is: where are the four still undiscovered sun temples? They should be lying under the sand and are, almost certainly, within sight of the summits of the Abusir pyramids. But where?

The Step Pyramid on the boundary of day and night.

CHAPTER IV

The Royal Mother

Visitors to the royal cemetery at Giza, who stand awestruck in front of that wonder of the world, the Great Pyramid, are usually convinced that its owner, Khufu, was the greatest of the Egyptian pyramid-builders. He was not. That pre-eminence belongs to his father Sneferu, who built no less than four pyramids with a total volume that exceeds the work of Cheops by roughly one third. It was on the orders of Sneferu that the pyramid in Meidum, the Bent Pyramid, the Red Pyramid in Dahshur, and the small pyramid in Seila were raised toward the heavens. Altogether, an incredible 3.6 million cubic meters of stone! Sneferu, later represented by the Ancient Egyptians as a wise and beneficent king, founded the dynasty whose rule and whose feats were to make the deepest impression on the memory of generations succeeding each other on the banks of the Nile. It was an impression to which the sheer weight of the Giza pyramids undoubtedly contributed. The names of Sneferu, Khufu, Djedefre, Khafre, and Menkaure marked out the Fourth Dynasty's glorious path like milestones and it seemed that there could be no limit to its power. Nevertheless, the dynasty met with sudden decline and fall, and ended in circumstances still more obscure than those in which it attained power. The mysterious tomb, which in Arabic is called the Mastabat Fara'un, is that of the last ruler of the dynasty, Shepseskaf, and it represents a question mark at the end of a famous era. But besides Shepseskaf, there was another figure who came to the fore during the obscure and confused period which set in at the end of the Fourth Dynasty. This figure was that of Queen Khenthaus I. In almost every respect she is surrounded by mystery, beginning with her origins and ending with her unusual tomb. Nevertheless, with the progress of

Neferirkare's pyramid, showing the construction of its core (photo: Milan Zemina).

archaeological excavations, new information has come to light which makes it ever more apparent that this woman played a key role not only at the end of the Fourth Dynasty but also in the inauguration of the new, Fifth Dynasty.

When the Egyptian archaeologist Selim Hassan began archaeological research on the so-called 'Fourth Pyramid' at Giza in 1932, surprises followed in rapid succession. "The Fourth Pyramid," a mysterious two-stepped monument on the eastern margins of the Giza cemetery near the Great Sphinx, had attracted the attention of archaeologists as early as the 19th century. For a time it was even considered to be the tomb of the little-known pharaoh Shepseskaf mentioned above. In the 1930s, and shortly before Hassan's excavations, this was still the belief of such famous experts on the royal cemetery in Giza as Uvo Hölscher, the German archaeologist and architect (who led the investigations of the pyramid complex of the pharaoh Khafre), and the American Egyptologist and archaeologist George Andrew Reisner, whose name is inseparable from research on the pyramid complex of Menkaure and the cemetery that once held members of Khufu's family. The first surprise brought by Hassan's excavations was the discovery that the 'Fourth Pyramid' was not a pyramid at all but, originally, a rock-cut tomb of mastaba type extended by a superstructure which transformed it into a stepped monument. The second surprise was that it belonged not to a king, but to Queen Khentkaus, at that time unknown, but obviously important, since her tomb was so large and had no parallels among contemporary, or indeed any other, Ancient Egyptian tombs. To the archaeologists of the day, it seemed that light would eventually be shed on the mysteries surrounding Queen Khentkaus and the fall of the famous dynasty but, as it turned out, that was a very hasty presumption.

Even in its original form, Khentkaus's tomb at Giza was a remarkable and unique building. It was entirely carved out of a rock outcrop and its ground plan, surprising and unusual in tombs of mastaba type, was fundamentally a square of 45.50 x 45.80 meters. The exterior face of the side walls of the superstructure of Khentkaus's tomb were sloping at an angle of 74° and adorned with a pattern of niches, a motif taken up from Early Dynastic architecture which had mainly employed dried bricks, wood and light plant materials. The niches resembled stylized, symbolic apertures representing entrances to the tomb. They were set all around the tomb and this was related to the concept of ever-multiplying gifts offered to the spirit of the deceased remaining in the tomb.

At a later stage another step, built from limestone blocks, was added to Khentkaus's rock tomb. This extension was not square but rectangular in plan and oriented the north–south direction. It was not placed over the center of the original building but shifted markedly toward its western part and its roof was not flat, but slightly rounded to facilitate the run-off of rainwater. The entire two-stepped struc-

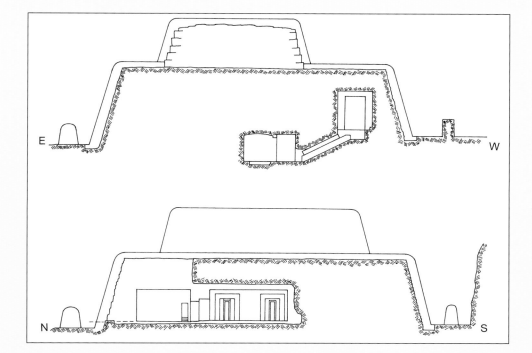

East–west and north–south sectional views through Khentkaus I's tomb (by V. Maragioglio and C. Rinaldi).

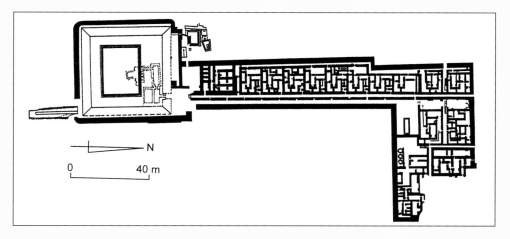

Plan of Khentkaus I's tomb complex at Giza, including the priests' settlement (by Selim Hassan).

ture, reaching a height of 17.5 meters, was finished with a smooth casing of smaller blocks of fine white limestone, which covered up even the decoration of the original tomb's outer walls. This unusual form of tomb did not come about by accident but, as we shall see, developed through the extraordinary circumstances accompanying the life of the queen.

The generally unconventional impression made by the outer appearance of the tomb is reinforced by its internal design. The mortuary cult chambers were concentrated in the southeastern part of the lower, older layer of the tomb. There were three of these and they were only accessible from the east, via a great gate of red granite originally equipped with heavy wooden doors. On the front face of the gate Selim Hassan found remnants of hieroglyphic inscriptions with the partially preserved tit-

View of Khentkaus II's pyramid complex
from the summit of Neferirkare's pyramid
(photo: Kamil Voděra).

ulary, name, and a tiny image of the queen. Of the original relief decoration of the walls of the three cult chambers—which are linked in a series from south to north—only a few fragments have survived; among them is a remnant of the so-called false

door, the symbolic passage between this world and the other world, which was set into the western wall of the northernmost chamber.

The underground part of the tomb was laid out in a way that in some respects resembles the substructure of Menkaure's pyramid. The similarity perhaps reflects something more significant than the proximity of these monuments in time, but its meaning is now obscured—partly because of the damage that has been done to these rooms. The underground part—a large antechamber, several narrow magazines, and above all the burial chamber—was devastated and pillaged by thieves in ancient times, evidently repeatedly. Of the sarcophagus in which the queen's mummy was once interred only tiny fragments have been found.

Reconstruction of a floral ornament in greenish-blue and black glazed faience from a symbolic vessel which once belonged to the burial equipment of Khentkaus II (by R. Landgrafová).

The tomb complex was, however, much larger than this description suggests and it included other archaeologically important features. Among them was a long narrow trench at the southwest corner of the tomb which originally contained the funerary boat by which the spirit of the deceased was to depart for the other world and float across the sky. At the northeast corner of the tomb there was a pool that was used for purification ceremonies and perhaps even during the mummification of the dead queen. The most noteworthy element was, however, the residential area in front of the anterior, eastern wall of the tomb. This contained the dwellings of the priests who maintained the mortuary cult of the queen in the period of the Fifth and Sixth Dynasties.

Khentkaus's whole complex, in the broadest sense, also included a number of neighboring tombs which were the burial places of people connected with the queen either by family ties or mortuary cult duties. Khenkaus's two-step tomb became the center of a small but independent cemetery that grew up gradually on the eastern margins of the Giza necropolis. From the archaeological viewpoint this is a remarkable phenomenon; elsewhere in the Giza necropolis it is a demonstrable pattern only in the case of rulers, whose pyramid complexes always represent the centers of satellite cemeteries of relatives, courtiers, officials, and priests—everyone, in short, who desired, and was entitled, to be close to his or her sovereign after death.

The siting of Khentkaus's tomb very close to Menkaure's valley temple is a fur-

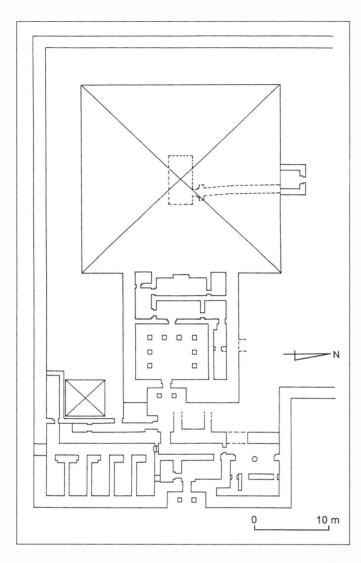

ther indication of a possible close relationship between the two individuals. This is a possibility that can only be strengthened by the discovery in Menkaure's valley temple of a fragment of a stone stele with a damaged hieroglyphic inscription which, according to some Egyptologists, might suggest that Khentkaus was the pharaoh's daughter.

Among the many extraordinary archaeological discoveries from Khentkaus's tomb complex, one in particular produced amazement and even a sensation. This was the inscription on a fragment of the granite gate—which has already been mentioned—which contained the never before documented title of a queen. Its discovery immediately raised a fundamental controversy among Egyptologists since, from a grammatical point of view, two interpretations were possible. Some translated the title as "Mother of the Two Kings of Upper and Lower Egypt," while others rendered it as "King of Upper and Lower Egypt and Mother of the king of Upper and Lower Egypt." The historical circumstances of the two suggested interpretations of one and the same title are essentially different. The first interpreta-

Plan of Khentkaus II's pyramid complex at Abusir (by Peter Jánosi).

Following pages: View of the pyramid complex of the royal mother Khentkaus II from the southwest (photo: Kamil Voděra).

tion was put forward by Vladimir Vikentiev, the Russian Egyptologist and émigré who at that time lived in Cairo, and the second by the Austrian Egyptologist Hermann Junker who at just that period had started the ambitious Austrian excavations in the cemeteries lying in the shadow of Khufu's pyramid. It is paradoxical that Vikentiev's opinion prevailed for such a long time when the discoverer of Khentkaus's tomb, Selim Hassan, had inclined immediately to Junker's interpretation. This was perhaps a result of the influence of the Westcar Papyrus, according to which the first three Fifth Dynasty rulers were brothers.

On the basis of all the data gathered during excavations, Selim Hassan drew remarkable—and perhaps rather hasty—historical conclusions. He considered the shape of the tomb, and especially the second step which resembled a huge sarcophagus, to be similar to Shepseskaf's Mastabat Fara'un. From this formal resemblance he deduced that Khentkaus and Shepseskaf, two figures from the last years of the Fourth Dynasty, had been married. Moreover, he saw in the shape of both tombs, so ostentatiously differing from the pyramid form which prevailed for royal tombs of the period and representing an almost a "religio-political" obligation, an expression of opposition by the ruling royal line to the ever-growing influence of the solar religion and the might of the priesthood of Re. He inferred that, after the

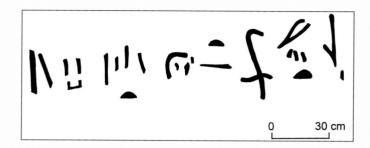

death of her husband, Khentkaus finally bowed to the priests of Re and was even forced to marry their High Priest, Userkaf, with whom she then founded the Fifth Dynasty. She refused, however, to be buried next to her second husband and so built her own tomb at Giza in the eternal resting-places of her famous royal ancestors.

Red painted mason's inscription on a block in the northeast corner of the foundation platform of Khentkaus II's pyramid. The title of "King's wife" preceding Khentkaus II's name was additionally complemented by the title of "King's mother." Obviously, the construction of the monument begun by the Queen's consort was later finished by her son.

As might be expected, Selim Hassan's researches and his theory attracted not only much attention but also mixed reactions from the scholarly community. One of the first to make a stand was Ludwig Borchardt. Having spent long years of archaeological research in the neighboring necropolis at Abusir, Borchardt immediately realized that the name of queen Khentkaus was familiar to him. The name Khentkaus, preceded by the title "Royal Mother," appeared on several fragments of papyri which had earlier been discovered in Abusir and which, it was later ascertained, had made up part of the archive of the pyramid complex of the Fifth Dynasty pharaoh Neferirkare (see below, Chapter VI). Not only these fragments of papyri, but also a number of other archaeological finds, such as an alabaster offering table with the remains of an inscription bearing the titles and name of the queen, provided indirect evidence for the cult of a queen mother named Khentkaus at Abusir. A fragment of an inscription on a piece of relief from Mertjesefptah's tomb at Abusir even makes express mention of Khentkaus's mortuary temple, which was evidently located somewhere in the Abusir cemetery. The historical conclusions drawn by Borchardt modified Selim Hassan's theory in many respects. According to Borchardt, Shepseskaf was not of royal origin and gained power only thanks to his marriage to Khentkaus. Their two sons, Sahure and Neferirkare, became legitimate rulers and founded the Fifth Dynasty. The first Fifth Dynasty king, Userkaf, gained the throne only through the premature death of Shepseskaf at a point when the two legitimate heirs to the throne were too young to assume power. Borchardt's conviction that Sahure and Neferirkare were brothers was undoubtedly influenced by the adjustments to the relief decoration that he discovered during his research in Sahure's pyramid complex at Abusir (see above, p. 49).

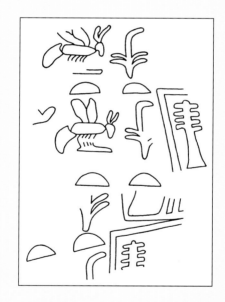

This inscription on a clay sealing from the reign of Djedkare mentions the unique title "Mother of the Two Kings of Upper and Lower Egypt ."

Yet, despite the efforts of Selim Hassan, Ludwig Borchardt, and some other Egyptologists, and indeed partly as a result of their theories and speculations, the reason for the fall of the Fourth Dynasty actually became ever more puzzling. For many

years after the initial discovery of the Khentkaus tomb, the subject seemed to have been exhausted. More than a quarter of a century later, however, at the beginning of the 1970s, the problem received fresh attention, this time from the German Egyptologist Hartwig Altenmüller, who re-examined the story of the Papyrus Westcar (see above, p. 70f.) from a literary-historical viewpoint. It occurred to Altenmüller that there could be a tangible connection between Queen Khentkaus and the celebrated Ancient Egyptian literary work preserved in the Westcar Papyrus. He expressed the opinion that the name Rudjdjedet, the earthly woman with whom Re had intercourse and who became the mother of the kings Userkaf, Sahure, and Neferirkare, was a pseudonym for none other than Queen Khentkaus. He then considered the coming to power of her sons as the rehabilitation of the adherents of the solar cult and as the resumption of the rule by the main branch of this pharaonic family.

Neither Altenmüller's theory nor various other attempts to explain the tangled circumstances of the fall of the Fourth Dynasty and rise of the Fifth were free of inconsistencies; nor did they meet with general acceptance within the scholarly circle. On the one hand there was an ever-growing tendency to regard the Royal Mother as a personal link between the two dynasties, though on the other hand she remained the symbol of a complex historical problem: the mysterious fall of a mighty royal line and the no less puzzling rise of a new ruling family and opening of a new epoch in Egyptian history. The confusing array of historical sources and of theories attempting to interpret them finally earned the question its own telling title in Egyptological literature: the "Khentkaus problem." Most Egyptologists came to believe that the "Khentkaus problem" could not be solved unless new information came to light. It was anticipated that any breakthrough would come either from as yet unpublished written sources, lying in the depositaries of world museums for example, or from new finds made during archaeological excavations. This second possibility is the one that has proved fruitful, since finds from the Czech archaeological excavations in Abusir in 1978 and the years following have apparently brought the desired new impetus to the hitherto stagnant discussion of the "Khentkaus problem."

It is puzzling that, during his work at Abusir, Ludwig Borchardt did not pay more attention to the ruins of a large building near the south side of Neferirkare's pyramid. Borchardt did, it is true, initiate trial digging, but he suspended further work on the site because he was convinced that the building was a twin mastaba and so an object having no priority in his archaeological research. This was undoubtedly a premature conclusion. The shape of the building, its conspicuous location and orientation by reference to Neferirkare's pyramid, its clear east–west alignment and several other features evident even from a superficial survey pointed in quite a different direction. They suggested that we are not dealing here with a twin mastaba but with a small pyramid complex, probably belonging to Neferirkare's wife and consisting of a modest pyramid with a temple in front of its eastern face. One example is the limestone block discovered in the 1830s at Neferirkare's pyramid by the British engineer and scholar John Shae Perring, to whom Egyptology is indebted for the earliest comprehensive set of descriptions and plans of pyramids. On this block, in red and in a cursive type of writing, was the inscription, "The King's Wife Khentkaus." A further example is another limestone block, found about fifty years ago in the village of

Red painted limestone pillars with the remains of hieroglyphic inscriptions containing the name and titles of Queen Khentkaus II (photo: Milan Zemina).

Abusir by the Egyptian archaeologist Edouard Ghazouli. It had apparently been dragged there from the ruins of Neferirkare's pyramid temple. Preserved on the block was the remnant of a scene in low relief depicting the royal family. Next to the Pharaoh Neferirkare and his eldest son Neferre (see illustration on p. 54) it shows and names "The King's Wife Khentkaus." Archaeological excavations in the area of the ruins of the mysterious building could therefore be initiated, in the second half of the 1970s, in the generally justified assumption that it was probably the small pyramid complex of Neferirkare's queen, Khentkaus.

The very first days of the Czech excavation work not only confirmed this theory, but also brought wholly unexpected discoveries. What began to emerge from the mil-

Reconstruction of the inscription on a fragment of relief with the titularies of Niuserre and Khentkaus II (by Jolana Malátková).

Detail of a picture of Khentkaus II on a pillar at the original entrance to the queen's mortuary temple at Abusir. The queen is wearing a vulture headdress and holding in her hands a papyrus scepter and an ankh (by Jolana Malátková).

Detail of a picture of the queen, Khentkaus II, with the uraeus on her forehead. Mortuary temple of the queen in Abusir (photo: Milan Zemina).

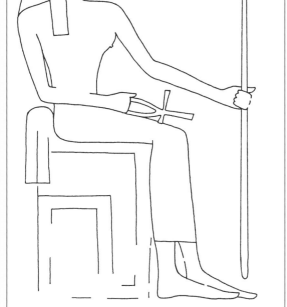

lennia-old sand deposits, both literally and figuratively, was not only a previously unknown pyramid complex but also an unknown chapter in the history of Ancient Egypt. It was very quickly confirmed that this was a pyramid connected to a mortuary temple, and it was also demonstrated that the whole building complex had been built and then reconstructed in several phases and that the history of its owner Queen Khentkaus was very much more complex than had been imagined.

Construction of the tomb in the form of a pyramid had undoubtedly commenced during the reign of Neferirkare and, as the remains of a cursive inscription on a limestone block in the masonry of the lower part of the monument showed, it had been destined for "The King's Wife Khentkaus." Construction work had, however, been interrupted shortly after its beginning, very probably owing to the king's death. After a break of perhaps two or three years (see above, p. 58f.), the building was completed. On the masonry blocks belonging to this second building stage, however, the original title of the owner of the pyramid, "king's wife," was replaced by a new one—"king's mother." Apparently, the construction of the monument started by the queen's husband was completed by a son of the queen.

On completion, the pyramid was perhaps 17 meters high, with sides 25 meters long and walls with an angle of inclination of 52°. The remains of the pyramid that have survived to this day reach a height of perhaps four meters. In the devastated burial chamber underneath the pyramid, no demonstrable fragments of the queen's physical remains have been discovered (that is, if we do not count a few shreds of linen bandaging which perhaps once swathed a mummified body). A similarly indirect piece of

evidence is the small fragment of a sarcophagus made of red granite found in the ruins at the foot of the pyramid.

The mortuary temple, built in front of the eastern face of the pyramid for cult reasons, was constructed in two major building phases. The first-phase temple was modest in dimensions although built out of limestone blocks. This earlier "stone phase" of the temple was so extensively destroyed by ancient stone thieves that today it is very difficult to reconstruct its original design in all details. The entrance to the temple was originally from the east, near the southeastern corner and decorated with twin pillars—limestone monoliths colored red and bearing on the exterior side a vertical hieroglyphic inscription in sunk relief with the queen's titulary, name, and picture. The front, or eastern half, of the temple was taken up by an open court decorated with similar pillars. The center of the queen's mortuary cult was in the western part of the temple in an offering hall with an altar and false door made of red granite. The false door was embedded in the western wall of the chamber and directly adjoined the pyramid. In front of it offerings would be placed by the mortuary priests. Beside the offering hall and in the westernmost part of the temple were three deep niches in which there originally stood wooden shrines with statues of the queen. A staircase in the southwest corner of the temple gave access to the temple's roof terrace on which the priests would conduct astronomic observations and certain ceremonies day and night.

The rooms in the western part of the temple were decorated with scenes and inscriptions in colored low relief. The temple's so-called 'decorative scheme' covered an astoundingly wide array of subjects, for example scenes of sacrifice, agricultural work, processions of personified funerary estates bearing offerings to the queen, and others. Among them there are also exceptional themes, such as a scene, unfortunately preserved only in several small fragments, probably depicting the ruler Niuserre and members of his family standing in front of the royal mother. On the fragment with the scene, just as on some other limestone fragments of reliefs and clay sealings, the queen's name is preceded by a title which is identical to the historically unique title of the Khentkaus buried in the step tomb at Giza: "Mother of the Two Kings of Upper and Lower Egypt" or "King of Upper and Lower Egypt and Mother of the King of Upper and Lower Egypt"! The remains of the inscription on the one pillar still standing in the temple court brought another unexpected surprise. The vertical hieroglyphic inscription with remnants of titles and the name Khentkaus terminates in a picture of the queen sitting on the throne and holding a *wadj*-scepter in her hand. The queen's brow is adorned with a cobra rearing to attack, the uraeus. At the time when the queen lived, the right to wear the uraeus on the forehead was the exclusive privilege of the ruling sovereign or of the gods. The ruler was in any case a god, according to the ideas of Ancient Egyptians—the only god living on earth among men. However, it cannot be excluded that the uraeus on the queen's forehead only indicates that the northern half of the courtyard in which the pillar stood was under the symbolical protection of the Lower Egyptian cobra goddess Wadjet. It is a significant addition to the queen's iconography, too. Be that as it may, this image of the queen with the uraeus was not to be the last of the surprising discoveries made during the archaeological uncovering of Khentkaus's pyramid complex.

According to the original plan, the pyramid and the stone mortuary temple should have been enclosed by a high wall built of limestone blocks. However, construction of the surrounding wall was never completed and such parts as had been erected were partially dismantled during the reconstruction and extension of the pyramid complex. The materials obtained from the original wall were used in the building of a diminutive so-called cult pyramid near the southeast corner of the older stone part of the temple. Reconstruction also included the basic extension of the temple towards the east. A new monumental entrance, again adorned with twin limestone pillars, was erected, this time precisely on the east–west axis of the pyramid complex. A small stone basin immediately by the entrance reminded the visitor of the duty of ritual purification before entering the temple. The spacious entrance hall was an important crossroads because it allowed access to a group of five magazines in the southeast corner of the extended part of the temple and to a group of domestic rooms in the northeastern corner; finally, towards the west, it gave access to the so-called "intimate" part of the temple containing the cult rooms. Limestone blocks were not used for the extension of the temple but, this time, the much more economical material of mud bricks. The mud brick walls were, of course, plastered and whitewashed, and sometimes adorned with paintings which at first sight and for a limited time softened the contrast between the effect of the two different building phases.

The meaning of the entire reconstruction project lay in a fundamental change of the conception behind the queen's pyramid complex. Originally an appendage of the great pyramid complex of Neferirkare, it became the architecturally and functionally "independent" tomb of a person whose rank was similar to that of a ruler. The fragments of papyri discovered in Khentkaus's pyramid complex indicate that there were at least sixteen statues of the queen standing in her mortuary temple.

The mortuary cult of Queen Khentkaus lasted, if in gradually diminishing form, for perhaps three centuries up until the end of the Sixth Dynasty. During the ensuing first Intermediate Period and disruption of state power, Khentkaus's pyramid was pillaged. Centuries went by and the abandoned, half-ruined, sanded-up pyramid complex became a convenient quarry from which, as early as the Nineteenth

Dynasty, stone was taken for building other tombs not far away. Individual stone-cutters built simple dwellings from fragments of stone within the ruins of the temple.

The surprising discovery of Khentkaus's pyramid complex at Abusir showed that there were two royal mothers named Khentkaus who lived almost at the same time, separated perhaps by one generation only. At the same time, however, it invested the whole series of historical problems known as the "Khentkaus problem" with a new urgency. In particular, two basic questions came to the fore:

1. Were the two queens who bore the rare title of "Mother of the Two Kings of Upper and Lower Egypt" / "King of Upper and Lower Egypt and Mother of the King of Upper and Lower Egypt," the Khentkaus, from Giza and the Khentkaus from Abusir, one and the same person, or were they two different people?

2. What was the real—or intended—meaning of this unusual title?

Thorough investigation of this problem seemed to demand, if this was at all possible, a re-examination of the archaeological monuments discovered by Selim Hassan during his research on the step tomb of Queen Khentkaus at Giza. The individual finds that Hassan had not publicized were lying, long forgotten, in some archaeological storehouse in Giza or in the depository of the Egyptian Museum in Cairo and it was not feasible to get hold of them again. What remained was only the tomb itself and especially the section in which the remains of inscriptions were still to be found, primarily on the fragment of the granite gate. Careful examination of this inscription, when undertaken with an eye to the information gained in Abusir, nonetheless led to a surprising discovery. Selim Hassan had overlooked a few very small but enormously important pictorial details! Just as at Abusir, at the end of the inscriptions on Khentkaus's granite gate at Giza there is a picture of the queen under her title. On the north and south parts of the gate the queen is depicted sitting on a throne. The picture of her on the northern section is damaged but, on the southern section, the picture is complete. Examination of the complete picture showed that to the queen's head, with its long wig, had been added the so-called vulture diadem, the ornament of Egyptian queens and goddesses, and also a short ritual beard evenly trimmed at the bottom. The ritual beard, fastened to the pharaoh's face, was of course the exclusive privilege of ruling sovereigns. To the queen's hand, placed on her breast, had been added a *hetes*-scepter! There is no

Line drawing of the facing picture of Khentkaus I (by Jolana Malátková).

Opposite:
Detail of an inscription on a fragment of the granite gate in front of the southeast corner of the tomb of Khentkaus I at Giza: a vulture headdress, a beard and a scepter were later added to the picture of the queen sitting on the throne (photography by Miroslav Verner).

doubt that all these changes to the queen's portrait were made additionally, possibly during the reconstruction of her Giza tomb into a two-step building.

The unexpected discovery at Giza and the no less unexpected new archaeological materials revealed at Abusir have completely changed our view of the "Khentkaus problem." Because the unsual title was thought to have belonged exclusively to Khentkaus I from Giza, when the Czech team commenced the excavation in the pyramid complex of Khentkaus II at Abusir in the late 1970s, and when the first fragments of inscriptions with the title were brought to light, everything seemed to be relatively clear and simple: The monument under excavation at Abusir was thought to have been the tomb of another queen of the same name, Khentkaus II and, at the same time, a sort of a cult place for the famous queen mother, Khentkaus I, buried in Giza. However, as the excavation advanced, and different kinds of archaeological and epigraphical materials accumulated, it became obvious that everything was much more complex and difficult than it first appeared. The simple explanation that there was only one queen mother Khentkaus who bore the title became untenable.

The examination of the architectural remnants of the pyramid complex of Khentkaus II did not provide any unequivocal evidence that there was a special part of the building, for instance a room or a false door, reserved for Khentkaus I; neither did the evidence reveal any traces of a cult designed specifically for her. Moreover, the examination of all available written documents—reliefs, sealings, and papyri found in Khentkaus II's pyramid complex, the papyri from Neferirkare's mortuary temple and, finally, the inscriptions from the Abusir tombs of priests engaged in the cult of the queen mother—showed that they all referred to Khentkaus II from Abusir. There was thus no support for the theory that Khentkaus I from Giza had a cult also in Abusir. As surprising as it may seem, there were two queen mothers, separated in time by one or two generations, who held the same unusual title. Each of them enjoyed high esteem and a high level cult in the place of her burial.

The answer to the remaining question about the meaning of the unusual title held by both queens can—at least in the case of Khentkaus II—be inferred, to a certain extent, from the available historical materials from Abusir. These materials surely indicate that Khentkaus II had two sons who became kings, Neferefre and Niuserre, thus giving some *raison d'être* for the explanation of the title as "The mother of two kings of Upper and Lower Egypt." These materials also indicate that some rivalry might have existed between the royal families of Sahure and Neferirkare (see above p. 58f.). According to one of the possible scenarios for the events following Sahure's death, the king's eldest son Netjerirenre, the potential heir to the throne, either might have died before his father or, alternatively, may have been a minor. Perhaps it was this situation that facilitated Neferirkare's claim to the throne.

Neferirkare's reign, however, was not long enough to stabilize the political situation completely in favor of his family. Moreover, the premature death of Neferirkare's successor, Neferefre (see Chapter V), could have permitted one of Sahure's sons an opportunity to launch a claim to the throne (perhaps as the ephemeral king Shepseskare) at the cost of the claim of Niuserre, the younger son of Neferirkare and Khentkaus II. In such a situation we might see the emerging importance of Niuserre's mother, Khentkaus II. The role she could have played in Niuserre's ascension to the throne would then explain her high esteem and the additional enlargement and upgrading of her mortuary cult by Niuserre. It is not excluded that in this complicated dynastic situation, Niuserre was supported by some influential courtiers and high officials, for instance by his later son-in-law and vizier, Ptahshepses (see Chapter VII).

In the case of Khentkaus I, the reconstruction of the events surrounding the queen's life are much more nebulous. She, too, was probably mother of two men who successively became kings, but who they were we do not know with certainty. There are several possible options, including Shepseskaf, Thamphthis, the mysterious last king of the Fourth Dynasty, Userkaf, Sahure, and Neferirkare. In some way, and regardless of all the new archaeological discoveries, the problem of Khentkaus I still remains unsolved.

Fragment of a butchering scene from the temple of Khentkaus II (photo: Milan Zemina).

CHAPTER V

The Secret
of the Unfinished
Pyramid

P artly submerged in sand and almost coalescing with the surrounding
desert terrain is the lowest step of a pyramid core that lies only a few
dozen meters southwest of Neferirkare's pyramid. For a long time it
represented what was, for Egyptologists, one of the mysteries of the
Abusir cemetery. Some attributed the building to the little-known
Fifth Dynasty pharaoh Neferefre, while others considered it the work of the still
lesser-known ruler of the period, Shepseskare (see above p. 58). There were also
those who hesitated to make any identification of its owner. They all agreed, however, that it was an unfinished pyramid and that, abandoned shortly after work had
commenced,it never served the purpose for which it had been planned and that
nobody was buried in it. It acquired the name of the Unfinished Pyramid at Abusir
and, apart from a few occasional visitors to this forgotten corner of Memphite
necropolis, nobody expressed any interest in it.

The Unfinished Pyramid became a priority interest of the Czech Egyptological
expedition of Charles University in Prague when in 1974 the Czech team obtained
the concession which allowed it to carry out archaeological research in an extensive
area south of Neferirkare's and Niuserre's pyramid complex. There were several reasons for the interest. Above all it was just at this time that papyri from the archive of
Neferirkare's mortuary temple were published by Paule Posener-Kriéger in the series
of the French Institute of Oriental Archaeology in Cairo. In one of the small remnants
published was a fragmentary allusion to Neferefre's mortuary temple and to the provision of a contribution to Neferirkare's mortuary cult. This allusion indirectly confirmed the existence of Neferefre's tomb and a mortuary temple somewhere near

Uncovering the
secrets of the Abusir
necropolis (photo:
Kamil Voděra).

Neferirkare's pyramid complex and which had, moreover, to be at Abusir. Evidence of another kind, but likewise relating to Neferefre, was a limestone block with the remains of relief decoration discovered not in Neferirkare's pyramid temple, from where it had originally come, but in Abusir village, where it had been used in the construction of a house. On the block was a partially preserved scene depicting Neferirkare's family and indicating that the ruler's eldest son was called Neferre, "Re is beautiful." It is more than probable that this Neferre and the later pharaoh Neferefre, Neferirkare's successor, were one and the same person. After ascending the throne, the prince simply slightly altered his name to Neferefre, "Re is his beauty," which expressed the status of a pharaoh more appropriately.

Another significant factor was the siting of the Unfinished Pyramid in the cemetery—it was clearly located as the third in a series, after Sahure's and Neferirkare's. The pyramids at Abusir, just as at Giza, were not positioned in the cemeteries randomly but in accordance with a particular scheme that is not yet understood in all its aspects. The fundamental axis of the cemetery at Giza was a line linking the southeast corners of the pyramids, while at Abusir it was a line linking the pyramids' northwest corners. Both lines, the axes of the pyramid cemeteries at Giza and at Abusir, converge towards a point that lies at Matariya, an eastern suburb of modern Cairo. In ancient times this was the site of the temple of Re and the famous center of the sun cult, *Iunu*, in Greek Heliopolis. It is possible that this was the "fixed point" of the world of the pyramid-builders. The positioning of the Unfinished Pyramid was such that, even before excavation work commenced, it could be anticipated that it belonged to Neferirkare's direct successor, which in normal circumstances would very probably be his eldest son Neferre, the later Neferefre.

The written evidence for the existence of Neferefre's mortuary temple—and a mortuary cult presupposed the existence of a tomb—and likewise the well-grounded belief that it was Nefrefre who built the Unfinished Pyramid, led to a single conclusion: despite its appearance and the negative results of the trial digging carried out there by Borchardt at the beginning of the century, the Unfinished Pyramid must once have been a real pharaoh's tomb. With this working hypothesis, research commenced at the end of the 1970s with the aim of finally revealing the secret of the Unfinished Pyramid.

The first step on the road to understanding the Unfinished Pyramid was geophysical surveying. In view of the particular condition of the terrain and the data required, the method chosen from the varied list of geophysical techniques was that of magnetometry. It was most intensively applied to the extensive sand plain, virtually indistinguishable from the surrounding desert, in front of the eastern wall of the Unfinished Pyramid. The results of this geo-magnetic measuring were rapid, unambiguous, and surprising. It was ascertained that under the sand in the lay a huge, highly articulated building of mud bricks, with a basic outline, seen from above, in the shape of the letter "T". This shape is characteristic of the basic layout of mortuary temples in the Fifth and Sixth Dynasties.

Archaeological excavations, precisely and rapidly targeted on the basis of the results of geophysical measurement, soon definitively confirmed the existence of a mortuary temple. It was demonstrated that the building complex dominated by the Unfinished Pyramid was indeed the tomb of the pharaoh Neferefre. Ludwig Borchardt had, in fact, been within inches of this discovery at the beginning of this century. He did not wish entirely to ignore the Unfinished Pyramid on the western margin of the Abusir cemetery and so he carried out trial digging. As an experienced archaeologist and expert on pyramids he decided to dig a trench in the deep open ditch which ran from the north into the center of the monument and at the bottom of which, in the case of a completed tomb, it would be natural to assume the existence of a passage leading to the sarcophagus chamber. He dug a trench several meters deep in the rubble that filled the ditch right up to its upper edge, but he did not reach the passage or its remains. This negative result confirmed to him the belief that he was dealing with a rough, unfinished building consisting of no more than the lowest step of a pyramid core, and that inside it work had never even started on the construction of the passage giving access from the north, the passage blockade (a stone portcullis),

The head of Neferefre is shielded from the back by the outspread wings of the falcon god Horus, whose earthly incarnation the pharaoh was considered to be. The statue thus very eloquently expresses the pharaoh's exceptional position and universal power (photo: Kamil Voděra).

View of the
Unfinished Pyramid
from the summit
of Neferirkare's
pyramid, just before
excavations were
started (photo: Milan
Zemina)

Following pages:
In several places the
mud brick masonry of
Neferefre's mortuary
temple has survived to
a surprising height
(photo: Kamil Voděra).

or on what is called the king's funerary apartment, i.e. the antechamber and the burial or sarcophagus chamber situated under the base-line of the pyramid, approximately in the vertical axis of the monument. The orientation of the passage was closely connected with the idea that after death the pharaoh's spirit would depart to the northern heaven to become one of the never-setting stars around the Polestar. The contrasting east–west orientation of the burial chamber—the sarcophagus at its western wall was, however, once again aligned northeast and the pharaoh's mummy laid in it with his head to the north and face turned to the east, to the rising sun—was dictated by the solar religion. This involved the belief that after death the pharaoh would become a member of the entourage of his father Re and together with him would float forever on the heavenly ocean.

Was it by mistake or merely by chance that Borchardt did not continue with his probe for at least another hour? Perhaps one meter lower than the point where he gave up his probe he would have made two archaeological finds under the rubble, and these would certainly have led him to a decision to investigate the Unfinished Pyramid and its surroundings thoroughly. Had he reached the bottom of the ditch, he would have discovered, partly still *in situ*, the huge blocks of red granite out of which was constructed the portcullis blockade in the passage giving access to the burial chamber. It would immediately have been obvious to an archaeologist as experienced as Borchardt that a substructure had been completed in its entirety, even though the pyramid superstructure above had never been finished. The second discovery was also not one that he could have missed. It was a cursive inscription

CAD reconstruction of a vertical section of Neferefre's burial chamber (by Jaromír Krejčí).

recorded in black on a block from the core of the Unfinished Pyramid that contains Neferefre's name in cartouche. The builder and owner of the Unfinished Pyramid would then have been known. Borchardt's premature negative conclusion had apparently consigned the Unfinished Pyramid to perpetual archaeological oblivion. This has made the possibility of correcting his conclusion after more than 70 years all the more pleasurable for the Czech team.

The excavations in Neferefre's pyramid complex proceeded, with intervals between individual archaeological seasons, throughout the 1980s and the 1990s. Some unexpected and in many respects unique archaeological discoveries have given us an entirely new view of the pyramid complex, the technical aspects of construction, the status of a royal tomb of that period, the organization of the royal mortuary cult, and so on. This has been made possible by the coincidence of two chance circumstances. On the one hand, an unfinished building offers an opportunity to look, as it were, backstage and throw light on many previously unexplained questions concerning the building of a pyramid. On the other hand, the appearance of this abandoned and sand-buried relic of a pyramid apparently held off whole generations of experienced medieval and modern tomb robbers and stone thieves.

On the site destined for the building of Neferefre's pyramid, which was already quite some way from the Nile Valley, the ground was leveled and bearings taken for the base of the future pyramid. In the middle of the base a rectangular trench was sunk, east–west in orientation, in which the underground parts of the future royal tomb were to be constructed. Then a deep ditch was dug down into the trench from

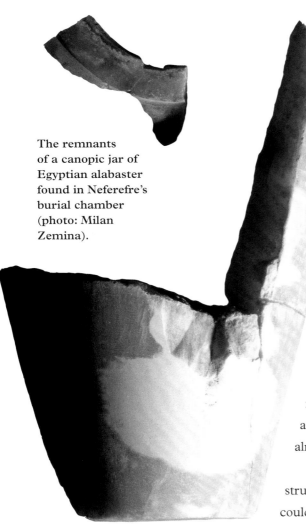

The remnants of a canopic jar of Egyptian alabaster found in Neferefre's burial chamber (photo: Milan Zemina).

the north; this was to be the basis of the passage leading down to the underground chambers. It is clear from the unfinished building that work on the underground section of Neferefre's pyramid was planned to begin a short time after the work on the masonry of the first, lowest step of the core of the section above ground. It was a logical approach, given the mode of construction of the gabled roof of the underground chambers. Originally, it had certainly been planned by the chief architect of Neferefre's pyramid to build, as in the earlier Abusir pyramids of Sahure and Neferirkare, a gabled roof which would have consisted of three layers, each layer made up of huge limestone blocks. However, the premature death of the king probably forced the architect to reduce the number of layers. Anyway, the procedure of the construction of the roof required the presence of compact masonry on the sides to which the huge blocks could be anchored. The construction of the gabled roof was therefore already to be found at the foundation level of a pyramid.

The untimely death of the young king, even before the construction of the descending corridor and the funerary apartment could be made, led to a drastic change in the original building project of the pyramid. All these underground rooms were hastily built and the large vacant space above the gabled roof of the king's funerary apartment was filled by lumps of stone and rubble arranged in diagonally running walls crossing over the pyramid's center. The hurriedly completed first step of the core of the pyramid, which resembled a truncated pyramid, was then faced with blocks of fine white limestone. The outer surface of the building, sloping at an angle of perhaps 78°, was carefully smoothed down. Finally what had been planned as a true pyramid became a truncated pyramid, in fact a sort of a mastaba with an atypical square ground plan. In appearance, the tomb resembled a hill, a stylized tumulus above a burial. This resemblance was not, of course, purely accidental. In one of the papyrus fragments found in Neferefre's mortuary temple there is evidence that his tomb was known as the

Fragment of Neferefre's left hand (photo: Milan Zemina).

"Mound" to those who built it and to those who served here in the pharaoh's mortuary cult. The upward-facing surface of the Mound was constructed in a very original way: the whole horizontal terraced roof of the mastaba was covered by a layer of clay several centimeters thick, into which was pressed coarse gravel collected from the surface of the surrounding desert. The roof terrace thus visually merged with the desert, and the weather over four and a half millennia left as little trace on it as on its desert surroundings.

Regardless of the large-scale damage caused to the monument by generations of stone robbers, the excavation of the pyramid's substructure brought a number of important discoveries. At the foot of the northern face of the monument, in front of the entrance to the descending corridor, the remnants of the so-called Northern Chapel were unearthed. The Chapel, built of mud brick, had originally been a small room with a vaulted roof. Only potsherds and tiny pieces of charcoal testified to the ceremonies once performed in this place following the king's burial and the sealing of the entrance to his tomb.

Approximately in the middle of the summarily built descending corridor lay the portcullis of red granite blocking the approach to the interior of the tomb. The construction of this portcullis is absolutely unique and has no parallel among the royal tombs of the pyramid age. Usually, the plug blocks would slide vertically—as was common at that time. Instead, for Neferefre, an ingenious system of pairs of stones with lugs and holes was used. This system was probably invented and used because the builders of Neferefre's tomb were aware of the fact that the monument could have been prone to easy attack by robbers from above.

From the king's funerary apartment only scanty remnants have survived, but these were significant enough to reconstruct the original plan of both rooms, the antechamber, and the burial chamber. Amongst the debris, moreover, some remains of Neferefre's burial were revealed: fragments of a red granite sarcophagus, fragments of alabaster canopic jars, fragments of offerings

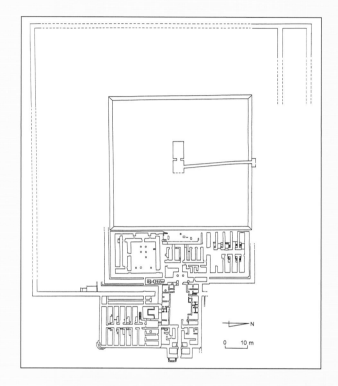

Plan of Neferefre's pyramid complex (by M. Švec and O. Vosika).

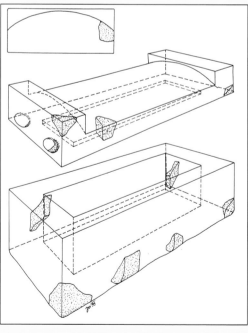

Reconstruction of Neferefre's sarcophagus (by Jolana Malátková).

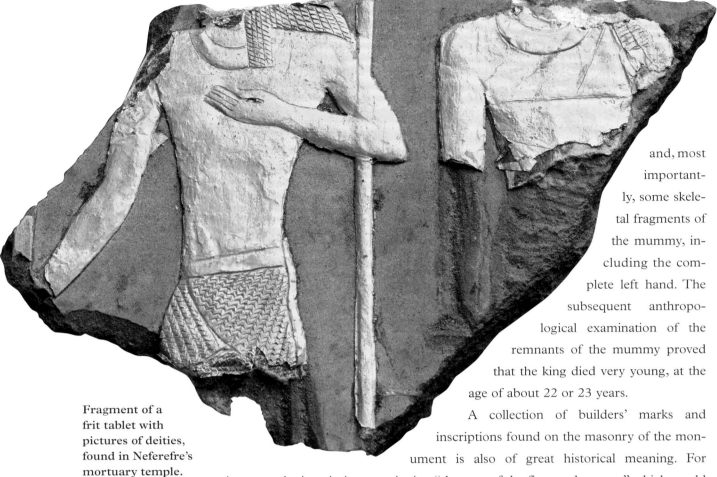

Fragment of a frit tablet with pictures of deities, found in Neferefre's mortuary temple. The raised figures of the deities were modeled with paste and then covered by thin gold leaf (photo: Jan Brodský).

and, most importantly, some skeletal fragments of the mummy, including the complete left hand. The subsequent anthropological examination of the remnants of the mummy proved that the king died very young, at the age of about 22 or 23 years.

A collection of builders' marks and inscriptions found on the masonry of the monument is also of great historical meaning. For instance, the inscription mentioning "the year of the first cattle count," which would correspond approximately to the second regnal year of the king, is very significant. It is very probable that in this year, or shortly afterwards, Neferefre died.

The unfinished state of the Pyramid has provided yet further significant archaeological testimony. It was long believed that the way in which pyramids were built was by the arrangement of the stone masonry of the stepped core into a system of slanted layers, inclined at an angle of 75° and leaning on a central stone spindle around the vertical axis of the pyramid. The effect, therefore, was of masonry arranged into a system of inner casings resembling the layers of an onion. The author of this theory was Richard Lepsius. It is interesting that it was on the basis of study of the Abusir pyramids, especially that of Neferirkare, that he developed his theory of the construction of pyramid cores. Ludwig Borchardt, who had investigated the three biggest Abusir pyramids, embraced the theory as well.

The Unfinished Pyramid, and the cleaning of thick layers of debris covering the remnants of the king's funerary apartment showed, however, a different structure of the pyramid's core than that was assumed by Borchardt. The outer face of the first step of the pyramid core was formed by a retaining wall made of huge blocks of dark gray limestone up to five meters long and well bound together. Similarly, there was an inner retaining wall built out of smaller blocks, and making up the walls of the rectangular trench destined for the underground chambers of the tomb. However, between the two walls, there were no accretion layers, just pieces of small poor-quality limestone sometimes packed "dry" or stuck together with clay mortar and sand; sometimes little compartments had been built of rough stone lumps and filled with rubble mixed occasionally with fragments of mud bricks and potsherds. As the core of Neferefre's pyramid, undoubtedly other large Abusir pyramids as well had therefore been constructed in this simple way. It was less demanding in terms of time and material but, at the same time, sloppier and less safe from the point of view of stability. The core was indeed modeled into steps but these were built in horizontal layers as described above. For this reason it is no wonder that today the Abusir pyramids,

An inscribed cylinder seal of limestone discovered in Khentkaus II's mortuary temple (photo: Milan Zemina).

long ago stripped of their casing of high quality white limestone and with their cores denuded and exposed to further human destruction and natural erosion, are now rather formless heaps of stone.

Upon Neferefre's death his heir was faced with a by no means easy task. It was his duty to complete the tomb and, as the new divine pharaoh, to prepare the burial of his equally divine predecessor. The site of the mortuary cult of a pharaoh was at that time usually a large temple erected in front of the east face of his pyramid, the face looking towards the rising sun. In the short time remaining before Neferefre's interment, however, it was evidently impossible even to think of building a standard temple consisting of an architecturally articulated complex planned on the basis of defined religious principles. For this reason a temple was hurriedly erected in front of the east face of the Unfinished Pyramid and on its east–west axis. The nucleus of the temple built of limestone blocks stood on the pyramid's base platform, which had been created by two layers of huge limestone blocks. This was because a five meter strip of free space on the platform remained around the pyramid, the space having been allowed in the original plan for completion of the pyramid's smooth limestone casing. The other parts of the temple were in mud brick.

In its initial phase the mortuary temple's design was simple and rectangular, with a north–south orientation. The limestone nucleus of the temple consisted of an open vestibule, where the priests carried out the essential purification rituals that were required on entry to the temple and, three other rooms. Of these the largest and most important was the offering hall. It was originally submerged in darkness and the false door, probably made of red granite, which represented the central place of the cult was embeded in its western. In front of the false door stood an altar on which offerings were placed and of which at least an imprint has remained in the paving of the chamber. It is possible that each of the two narrow rooms at the sides of the offering chamber originally contained what is known as a funerary boat. A small shaft under the temple's paving yielded the discovery *in situ* of a so-called foundation deposit consisting of symbolic vessels, a piece of fine dark gray clay used for the sealing, and the heads of a small bull and a bird sacrificed during the ceremonies connected with the foundation of the temple.

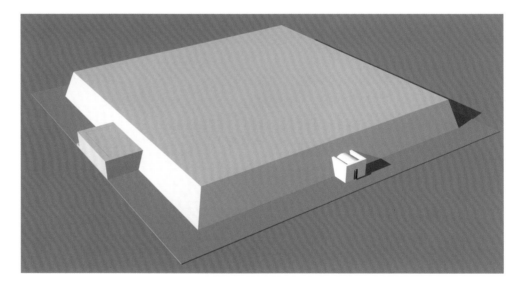

CAD reconstruction of Neferefre's tomb including the earliest stage of the king's mortuary temple (by Jaromír Krejčí).

As yet, we do not know with certainty who began to build the initial small mortuary temple for Neferefre and who, therefore, his direct successor was who ruled for a short time either immediately before or immediately after Neferefre. On two clay sealings, found close to the oldest Neferefre mortuary temple, Sekhemkhau, apears the so-called Horus name of an ill-attested king otherwise known as Shepseskare. Was Shepseskare, then, Neferefre's successor? We do not know but, if he was, it was only for a very brief period. In any case, when Neferefre's brother Niuserre, who was to rule for more than thirty years, ascended the throne, he confronted a series of difficult tasks. One of these was to complete, at least provisionally, the half-finished tomb complexes of the closest members of his family—his father Neferirkare, his mother Khentkaus II, and his brother Neferefre. The later phases in which Neferefre's temple was fundamentally extended and basically modified in design can certainly be ascribed to Niuserre. The building projects show signs of both improvisation and originality. The result was the emergence of a huge and architecturally unique tomb complex which in its design conception has no parallel among pyramid temples. It received the name "Divine are the souls [i.e. divine is the power] of Neferefre."

With the earlier building phase, there emerged a large temple with a rectangular ground-plan which stretched along the whole eastern side of the Unfinished Pyramid. With the exception of a few architectonic elements it was entirely built of mud bricks, a material much less durable than stone but representing a saving of time and money. The main axis of the earlier-stage temple was north–south in orientation; no other pyramid temple is aligned in this way, if we set on one side the older and in many respects dissimilar group of step pyramid complexes of the Third Dynasty and Userkaf's mortuary temple from the early Fifth Dynasty, which was atypically oriented as a result of particular topographical conditions. This unusual characteristic was undoubtedly a consequence of the fact that the architect was faced with the singular task of building a royal mortuary temple not in front of a pyramid—the standard type of royal tomb of the period—but in front of a mastaba, albeit one of markedly unusual design. The only possibility was to improvise, making a break with all the previous customs and more or less settled norms of royal funerary architecture.

The entrance to the second-stage temple lay in the middle of the eastern facade. It was adorned with two four-stemmed lotus columns made of white limestone; these held up an architrave placed crossways on which rested the wooden boards of a roof terrace. In the central part of the temple, between the columned entrance and the offering hall with the false door installed in the small stone first-phase temple, there was neither an entrance chamber, an open court, nor even a sanctuary with five niches and the pharaoh's cult statues—all features found in other pyramid temples. Instead the central part contained, besides the access passages, five large magazines in which probably the more valuable temple equipment used for cult ceremonies was originally stored. After damage due to a minor accidental fire in the western part of the temple two wooden cult boats were ritually buried and sprinkled with sand in one of these chambers. They were buried with piety, as is shown by about two thousand cornelian beads, perhaps originally strung on a thread, discovered around the boats. This isolated find has led us to reflect just how little we really know of the everyday religious and cult practices in Egypt at that time.

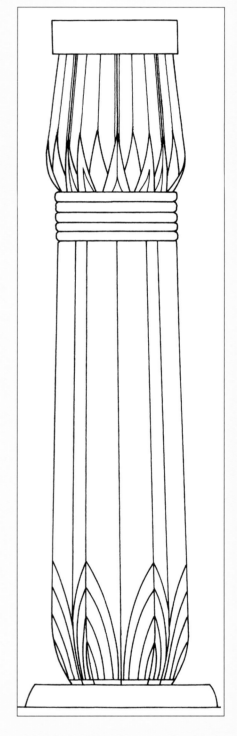

Reconstruction of a six-stemmed papyrus column from Niuserre's mortuary temple (by L. Borchardt).

The northern part of the earlier-phase temple was filled by ten large chambers—storerooms, originally on two stories. They were arranged in five pairs located opposite each other and accessible from a common passage. The number of rooms was not accidental. This is because the mortuary cult in the temple maintained a priesthood divided into five groups or *phylai* (see below, p. 143). In addition to papyri, somewhat mysterious fragments of frit tablets and faience ornaments have been discovered in these storerooms. The frit tablets with depictions of gods and the pharaoh accompanied by hieroglyphic inscriptions are encrusted with a white paste and covered with thin gold leaf. They perhaps originally adorned some cult objects and wooden boxes holding the precious pieces of temple equipment. In contrast, the faience ornaments probably decorated the large wooden symbolic vessels used during temple ceremonies. The storerooms likewise yielded discoveries of vessels made of diorite, alabaster, *gabbro* (a kind of volcanic rock), slate, limestone and basalt, practical and cult pottery, flint knives and blades, and other remains. The apparently modest clay sealings bearing the imprints of inscriptions from cylindrical seals have enormous scientific value. They come from the jar stoppers on vessels and fastenings on boxes containing cult objects, and from doors and even papyrus scrolls. The priests serving in Neferefre's temple, just like Ancient Egyptian officials in general, were obsessed by a bureaucratic longing continually to check and register everything and at every moment to have precise information on what was in the storerooms, who was responsible for it and what had to be obtained or released. Cheap, easily procurable clay, which could be molded without difficulty and stuck on the end of a string wound around a chest or the neck of a vessel and which could be imprinted with the text on the cylindrical seal entrusted to the hand of a responsible official, was the almost perfect means to fulfill this bureaucratic obsession. It is thanks to this mania that today we are able, from the seals bearing the names of kings and officials, gods, temples, palaces, and others, to reconstruct with great chronological precision the organization of the administration, economic relations, the mode of keeping accounts, and many other phenomena of great historical significance. The discoveries from Neferefre's temple have more than doubled the number of seals dating from Old Kingdom and so far known.

The greatest architectural and archaeological surprise, however, was brought by excavations in the southern part of the temple. Under a layer of sand, rubble, and fragments of mud brick almost four meters thick were buried the remains of a large columned hall—a hypostyle. It was an absolutely unexpected discovery since nothing similar had previously been found in any of the known mortuary temples in the pyramid complexes, or indeed in other monuments of the age of the pyramid-builders. The find was the first known archaeological evidence of a columned hall from

Head of a statue of Neferefre, which was damaged by fire. The pharaoh is wearing the nemes head-cloth and a long ritual beard is attached to his chin. Diorite. The head with the beard is 13.2 centimeters high. The statue is now in the Egyptian Museum in Cairo (JE 98180) (photo: Milan Zemina).

Ancient Egypt. The hypostyle hall was rectangular in design and oriented east–west. The space in the hall was divided up by four lines of five columns, aligned in the same east–west direction. Not one of the columns has survived but, from the imprint on one of the limestone bases, we can tell that they were designed to resemble sheaves of six lotus or papyrus buds. They were of wood, covered with a thin layer of stucco and multi-colored, and they supported the flat wooden ceiling of the chamber at a height of perhaps four meters. Nothing has survived of the roof either, although from remains of polychrome stucco discovered on the clay floor of the hall we can be almost sure that it was painted blue and decorated with gilded stars. The hall was undoubtedly originally sunk in shadow, as is suggested, for example, by the ceiling decoration. There can also be no doubt that important rites of the mortuary cult were performed there, as several archaeological finds suggest.

In the columned hall itself and in its immediate vicinity numerous fragments of statues of Neferefre made of diorite, basalt, limestone, reddish quartzite, and wood were discovered. Among them were six complete portraits of the pharaoh! The smallest and most beautiful of the statues, understandably in fragments and incomplete, was of rose-colored limestone and was originally about 35 centimeters high. It represented the young pharaoh, Neferefre, sitting on a throne and holding to his breast the mace, or *hedj*, the emblem of kingly power. The ruler's head, its brow originally adorned with a uraeus, was protected from behind by the outstretched wings of the falcon god Horus. The Egyptian pharaohs considered themselves the earthly incarnations of the highest god of the heavens, Horus, and the statue was therefore expressing, in an original fashion, the linking of earthly and heavenly might in the person of the pharaoh. Previously the famous diorite statue of the enthroned Khafre from his valley temple at Giza, now one of the most celebrated exhibits at the Egyptian museum in Cairo, was considered, together with Pepi I's statue, the only evidence of this conception in this type of statue. Other statues discovered in Neferefre's mortuary temple represent the ruler striding with the so-called white Upper Egyptian crown on his head and the sovereign's mace in his hand, or sitting on the throne and wearing on his head the pleated covering called the *nemes*.

The largest of the stone statues of Neferefre was approximately 80 centimeters in height. All these statues were characterized by perfect craftsmanship in relation to materials, and a masterly artistic shaping of the ruler's likeness and expression of his celestial kingly power. The largest of all the statues found was originally life-size and made of wood. Unfortunately no more than fragments of it survive: a part of the sole with the base, a ritual beard and a part of the hand with the thumb. It was probably this statue in particular which played an especially important part in the cult ceremonies in the columned hall, as is suggested by several fragments of

Bust of the pharaoh Neferefre, his head adorned by the nemes. The bust is a fragment of a statue that originally represented the ruler sitting on his throne. Basalt. The bust, 23.8 centimeters high, is now in the Egyptian Museum in Cairo (JE 98177) (photo: Kamil Voděra).

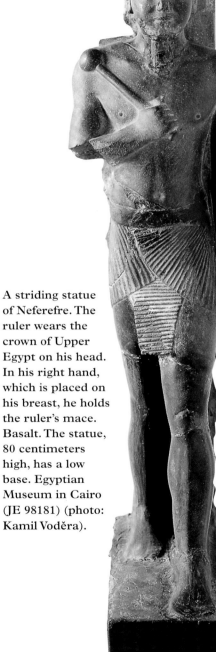

A striding statue of Neferefre. The ruler wears the crown of Upper Egypt on his head. In his right hand, which is placed on his breast, he holds the ruler's mace. Basalt. The statue, 80 centimeters high, has a low base. Egyptian Museum in Cairo (JE 98181) (photo: Kamil Voděra).

papyri from the temple archive. The discovery of Neferefre's statues, which are today on permanent exhibition at the Egyptian Museum in Cairo, represents in terms of extent what is so far the third largest find of royal sculpture from the Old Kingdom. This find is all the more valuable because it fills what has up to now been a perceptible gap in the recorded development of royal sculpture in Ancient Egypt in the third millennium BCE.

Yet further sculptures, however, were found in the hypostyle in Neferefre's mortuary temple; these were not of the ruler, but closely associated with him. They were small wooden statuettes of the so-called enemies of Egypt. They represented Asians, Nubians, and Libyans kneeling with their hands tied behind their backs. The statuettes may have originally adorned the royal throne or *naos* in which stood the statue of the pharaoh. The motif of the captured enemies kneeling before the pharaoh is a thoroughly royal motif linked with the Ancient Egyptian conception of the arrangement of the world and the status of the pharaoh within it. This was the reason why the motif of the captive enemies so often adorns objects around the pharaoh. Not only the statuettes of the captive enemies of Egypt but also many other archaeological discoveries—symbolic models of boats, fragments of stone vessels or faience decorations, clay seals and so on—are allowing us gradually to reconstruct the significance and function of the columned hall in Raneferef's mortuary temple.

The architectonic plan embodied the religious conception and made of the columned hall the place of the other world *par excellence*. Under the heavenly night canopy of the hall sheaves of lotuses (perhaps papyrus), symbol of resurrection, flowered in the form of the columns. The pharaoh, finding his image in a cult statue—and his various sovereign likenesses in his various statues—had made for himself an intimate world of eternal bliss, from which he could continue to govern the destinies of "the people of his time," exist as a living god on earth, and act as a mediator between the worlds of gods and men. This was the basic conception behind the cult which was practiced in the hall with the precision of a timetable of priestly services. It is also possible that the columned hall resembled the throne hall in a royal palace. To confirm this resemblance it would, of course, be necessary to find and archaeologically investigate at least one royal palace from the age of the pyramid-builders. Unfortunately, such a discovery still remains one of the unfulfilled goals of Egyptian archaeology.

While it is true that archaeological examples of royal palaces from the time of the pyramid-builders have not been found and are known only from contemporary Egyptian written records, Neferefre's tomb complex has nevertheless yielded remarkable testimony of a different kind. When the excavations in front of the Unfinished Pyramid were shifted further towards the southeast, another large building of mud brick began gradually to emerge from the sand and rubble. Like Neferefre's mortuary temple, it was built in two phases of construction, was rectangular in plan, and north–south in orientation. Its dimensions, orientation, and rounded outer corners indicate that it was not residential or economic but religious in character. Thorough archaeological research eventually brought its purpose to light: to serve the needs of the cult of Neferefre, a cult slaughterhouse for sacrificial animals had been built in the immediate vicinity of the pharaoh's mortuary temple! From the written records discovered, for example, the inscriptions on the vessels for fat or fragments of papyri in the temple archive, it was ascertained that this cult abattoir was named "the Sanctuary of the Knife." While this name had been known from other contemporary written sources, its interpretation had been the subject of dispute because archaeological evidence had been lacking.

Neferefre's "Sanctuary of the Knife" had a single, relatively wide entrance from the north through which the sacrificial animals, mainly cattle but also wild goats, gazelles and others, were led inside. These would then have been ritually slaughtered with the aid of sharp flint knives in the open courtyard in the northwest part of the slaughterhouse. In the chambers in the northeastern corner of the slaughterhouse the meat would then have been cut up on a wooden chopping board and prepared by heating. The rest of the abattoir—at least two thirds of the building—consisted of storage rooms. A staircase leading to a roof terrace suggests that this space, too, fulfilled a particular function in the context of the slaughterhouse; perhaps the meat would have been dried in the sun here. The great capacity of the storage areas of "the Sanctuary of the Knife" was initially rather puzzling, but only until there had been time for at least a general examination of the newly-discovered papyri of Neferefre's temple archive. On one of the fragments it was possible to read that on the occasion of the ten-day religious festivals thirteen bulls would be killed daily to supply the needs of Neferefre's mortuary cult. This means that during individual annual festivals and to meet the requirements of a single royal mortuary cult an unbelievable 130 animals would be killed! This figure testifies not only to the intensity of the cult and the number of people whose economic life would be linked simply with one mortuary temple and who would themselves consume the offerings made to the pharaoh's

Neferefre sitting on the throne. In his right hand, placed on his breast, he holds the ruler's mace. The pharaoh is dressed in a short skirt. A uraeus, probably made of gold, originally adorned his forehead. The statue, originally approximately 40 centimeters in height, has a low base. Rose limestone. Egyptian Museum in Cairo (JE 98171) (photo: Kamil Voděra).

spirit after completion of the ceremonies, but also suggests how great the material resources tied up—essentially unproductively—in the building of the huge tomb complexes and their long-term maintenance were. Undoubtedly this was one of the causes of the economic, political, and social decline of the Ancient Egyptian state at the end of the Old Kingdom.

"The Sanctuary of the Knife" served its purpose for a relatively short time. Already, during the reign of the Niuserre, the ruler who built it, Neferefre's mortuary cult was reorganized, the supplies of meat for the pharaoh's offering table were secured from elsewhere and "the Sanctuary of the Knife" became a storehouse. This change occurred at the point when the decision was taken to extend Neferefre's mortuary temple towards the east and alter its design to approximate more to the standard pyramid temple model of the period.

The last major building phase in the temple's development principally involved the construction of a new monumental entrance and a large open columned courtyard. The temple acquired the characteristic form of a "T" in its rough ground plan and the once independent "Sanctuary of the Knife" became an integral part of it. The monumental entrance was placed, as in the preceding building phase, on the east–west axis of the tomb complex. Its roof was supported by a pair of six-stemmed columns of fine white limestone in the form of bundles of papyrus stems. Just like the lotus, the papyrus was a plant of great symbolic significance in the religious conceptions of the Ancient Egyptians. In the time of the pyramid-builders dense papyrus undergrowth covered the great flats of the mud banks of the Nile. Papyrus rapidly renewed itself, was always green and fresh and therefore became a symbol of resurrection, eternal life, and permanent prosperity. Religious beliefs

Detail of the upper half of a statuette of a captive Asian chieftain discovered in Neferefre's mortuary temple. The chieftain is represented kneeling with hands bound behind his back. His shoulder-length hair is tied with a headband and he has a pointed beard. The statuette was originally inserted into a larger object, perhaps a throne or a naos. Wood, 15.5 centimeters high. Egyptian Museum in Cairo (JE 98182) (photo: Jan Brodský).

also influenced the design of the open courtyard, another place of important ceremonies for the royal mortuary cult. The courtyard was rectangular and oriented east–west in layout. Around its sides 24 columns supporting a flat wooden roof were arranged at regular intervals. Not a single column has survived and they have left only a few limestone bases, on one of which is the characteristic circular imprint of the shaft. The circular imprint suggests that the columns were of wood and fashioned to resemble date-palms—the symbol of fertility, abundance, and peace. This symbolic meaning was one of the reasons why the legendary palm grove in the venerable Lower Egyptian royal seat Buto became the mythical national cemetery of the Ancient Egyptians.

No vestige remains of the wall paintings that decorated the walls of the courtyard or of the stone, perhaps alabaster, altar that originally probably stood in the northwest part of the courtyard and on which offerings would be presented. At the latest at the beginning of the Sixth Dynasty, in the reign of Teti, the entrance to "the Sanctuary of the Knife" was walled up and the whole of this part of the temple was permanently taken out of commission. From papyri surviving from Neferefre's temple archive it can be inferred that even before this point, in the reign of Djedkare, the appearance and function of the columned courtyard had changed fundamentally. Irregular, sporadic, and even bizarre brick constructions of dwellings for the priests who served in the temple appeared in the area between the columns. The settlement of priests immediately inside the temple's columned courtyard further reduced the temple's status and accelerated its decay. From archaeological and written evidence it is clear that the cult in the temple died out at the end of the Sixth Dynasty under the long rule of Pepi II. During roughly the following two centuries of the so-called First Intermediate Period, which was characterized by the decay of central state power and by social unrest, Neferefre's mortuary temple and his tomb itself was robbed for the first time.

After the renewal of strong state power in the country at the beginning of the Middle Kingdom the cults in the Abusir

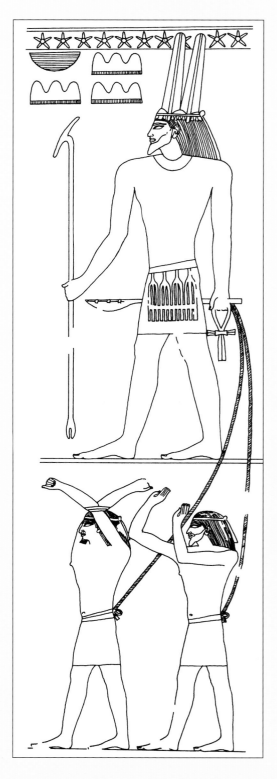

Two Asian captives led on the rope by the god Sopdu, the Lord of Foreign countries. Polychrome low relief in limestone from Sahure's mortuary temple at Abusir (by L. Borchardt).

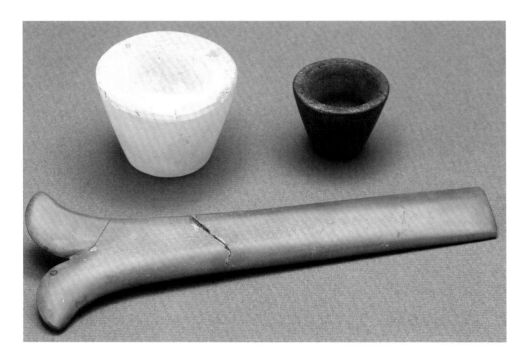

Peseshkef knife in the shape of a swallow-tail, conical limestone bowl, and conical basalt bowl. These were cult objects used in the ceremony of the Opening of the Mouth. The knife, made of gray-black slate, is 16.7 centimeters long, the limestone bowl is four centimeters high, and the basalt bowl is three centimeters high. They were all found in Neferefre's mortuary temple and are now in the Egyptian Museum in Cairo (JE 9730) (photo: Jan Brodský).

Flint knife and blades found in Neferefre's mortuary temple (photo: Jan Brodský).

royal mortuary temples, including Neferefre's, were temporarily resuscitated. It is from this period that there dates a remarkable interment discovered in a wooden sarcophagus of box type, richly decorated inside with religious texts. The burial pit for the sarcophagus was dug in the floor of a chamber in an already long abandoned and ruined "Sanctuary of the Knife." The man buried here was a hunchback, crippled as a result of severe tuberculosis of the bone. He was called Khuiankh and he was very probably one of the last of Neferefre's mortuary priests. Then once again, and this time for ever, Neferefre's tomb complex fell into oblivion.

Under the New Kingdom, the temple's destruction as a building began. Particularly in the earliest part of the temple thieves began to quarry away limestone blocks for new building works. Simple people from the villages in the nearby Nile Valley started to bury their dead in the temple area in primitive, anthropoid wooden coffins in the belief that the best final resting place was in the shadow of the mon-

uments of the mythical rulers and heroes of long ago. This common people's cemetery was abandoned as late as the beginning of the Roman era, roughly around the divide between BCE and CE. In the centuries that followed, the ruin of the Unfinished Pyramid, buried under the sand, apparently repelled rather than attracted the attentions of tomb-robbers. It is partly due to this fact that we owe the opportunity today to study one of the best preserved royal mortuary temple complexes of the Old Kingdom, to plunge into the secrets of the papyri of Neferefre's temple archive, and to admire the pharaoh's superb statues on exhibition at the Egyptian Museum in Cairo.

A view of Neferefre's pyramid complex under excavation (photo: Kamil Voděra).

Flooded palm grove near
the village of Kazrouni
on the way to Abusir
(photo Milan Zemina)

CHAPTER VI

The Testimony of the Papyrus Archives

Among the scanty Old Kingdom hieratic documents, the Abusir papyri undoubtedly occupy a very prominent position. At first sight, these fragmentary records of the Abusir pyramid temple administration and economy might seem unattractive and dull. However, their meaning for ancient Egyptian history is invaluable. Moreover, the intriguing circumstances of their discovery, and the tricks which fate played with them make of the Abusir papyri an apt subject for a romantic novel.

Today, papyrus only grows in newly established plantations (photo: Kamil Voděra).

Nobody can precisely identify the day on which a group of *sabbakhin*, the "fertilizer men" from the village of Abusir set out, as they had done so often before, for nearby pyramids on the desert plateau in order to dig there. It was, it seems, sometime in 1893 and the men were certainly not workers on archaeological excavations. The whole situation, indeed, was truly curious with no lack of historical dimension and paradox; the *sabbakhin* were merely one of its inseparable elements.

In the distant past, four and a half millennia ago when the pyramids were built, unending lines of workmen and bearers traveled up from the Nile Valley to the desert. They would not only carry or drag huge stone blocks large enough to amaze us even today, they would also carry up to the building-site the most valuable of the Nile's possessions—fertile clay. They would mix it with water and crushed straw and manufacture bricks directly at the building-site. The sun-dried bricks found multiple uses in the building of the pyramid complexes, especially when it was essential to economize or hurry. Sometimes whole temples at the foot of pyramids were built of these mud bricks. After the buildings were completed, smoothly plastered, whitewashed and richly decorated with colored pictures they looked, to begin with at least, as noble and timeless as the stone monuments beside them. Brick buildings, however, rapidly deteriorate. The mortuary cult and the traffic connected with it, sometimes lasting for a whole series of generations, in some cases slowed the decay and in others accelerated it. Another factor was the no less contradictory love of order among the mortuary priests; on the one hand, they were obsessed with ritual cleanliness but on the other they pushed heaps of refuse into back chambers and corners without scruple. This does not surprise or bother archaeologists who, on the contrary, are delighted by the huge layers of rubbish and disintegrated mud bricks which today cover large areas of the pyramid fields. These so-called "cultural layers," containing, in addition to disintegrated clay, rich organic ingredients, attract the attention not only of archaeologists but, long before them, of *sabbakhin*. For generations these scavengers have been accustomed to daily treks into the desert for the pyramids with hoes and baskets to search for and dig out the "clay" from the "cultural levels," bringing it back down to the Nile Valley to use as added fertilizer for their small fields and gardens on the edge of the eternally encroaching desert sands. The thousand-year cycle of the circulation of clay between the Nile Valley and the desert by the hands of men thus continues.

On that fateful day sometime in 1893, the Abusir *sabbakhin* were very successful. They found not only clay to fertilize their fields but also papyri—numerous fragments and larger pieces of scrolls. They rapidly and precisely appraised the rags of papyri with the black and sometimes red inscriptions that they had turned up with their hoes, and evaluated them from the point of view of possible profits on the

illicit market in antiquities. As was shown later, they carefully raked over the site of
the discovery and gathered up nearly all the papyrus fragments which they then
sold to Cairo dealers in antiquities. It was not long before the papyri turned up on
the Egyptian antiquities market. They were very rapidly snapped up by experts
who immediately realized their overall value. Some of the papyri ended up in the
Egyptian museum in Giza, whose collections were only at the beginning of the century transferred to the then recently completed and now central Egyptian museum
in Cairo. Others came into the possession of foreign Egyptologists, especially Henri
Edouard Naville and William Matthew Flinders Petrie. The remarkable journeys of
the papyri did not, however, end there.

At the end of the 1890s, German archaeological excavation commenced in the
remains of the great sun temple of the Fifth Dynasty king Niuserre to the north of
Abusir in the locality of Abu Ghurab. The German expedition was led by Wilhelm
von Bissing, but the excavation was directed by the then young architect and archaeologist Ludwig Borchardt. Borchardt had been interested in the Abusir pyramids for
some time and, in connection with the excavations at Abu Ghurab, he had developed
a particular interest in the pyramid of Niuserre, which had been identified and briefly

Mme. Paule Posener-Kriéger was present at the excavations in Neferefre's mortuary temple at Abusir at the moment that the most beautiful of Neferefre's statues was discovered (photo: Milan Zemina).

described more than sixty years before by the English scholar John Perring. It was very probably the chance discovery of the papyri mentioned above that led Borchardt to the firm decision to start extensive archaeological excavations at Abusir immediately upon finishing his work at Abu Ghurab.

The excavations at Abusir took place between 1900 and 1908. Before Borchardt began his excavation, a German Egyptologist named Heinrich Schäfer had attempted to locate the original site of the discovery of the papyri in just seven days of trial digging—without results. He searched around Neferirkare's pyramid, since the papyri clearly indicated Neferirkare's pyramid complex as the place of their origin.

Borchardt's first attempt to find other papyri in 1900 was likewise unsuccessful, despite his considerable archaeological experience, knowledge of local conditions, and rare ability to obtain valuable archaeological information from the native inhabitants. It was only in February 1903 that he managed to find several fragments of papyri, just a few square centimeters in size, in the ruins of Neferirkare's mortuary temple, in the storerooms east of the southeast corner of the king's pyramid. Borchardt had certainly expected to find a larger deposit of papyri, but it would be wrong to speak of a complete disappointment. Among the fragments was one which Hugo Ibscher, the celebrated papyri restorer from the Berlin Museum, managed to join together with a piece of papyrus found by the *sabbakhin* ten years before. The origin of the papyri and even the place in which the *sabbakhin* had found them was therefore conclusively established.

The Abusir papyri had generated great excitement in specialist circles, and world museums with large collections of Ancient Egyptian antiquities had expressed interest in them. For this reason they did not long remain in the hands of Naville, Petrie, and others who had come into contact with them and they ended up in London, Berlin, Paris and also, of course, in Cairo. In London they were acquired by two institutions—the British Museum and University College. Similarly, in Berlin some of the papyri are today to be found in the Staatliche Museen zu Berlin (the former East

Berlin) and some in the Staatliche Museen der Stiftung Preussischer Kulturbesitz (the former West Berlin). In Cairo they were simply shifted from one bank of the Nile to the other, from the former museum at Giza to the Egyptian Museum opened in the center of Cairo in 1900. The movements of the main state collections of Ancient Egyptian antiquities within the boundaries of modern Cairo were in fact rather more complicated. Originally, it was decided by the Egyptian government that the collection created in 1858 and located on the east bank of the Nile in the Bulaq quarter should be transferred to the Giza quarter on the west bank. Finally, the collection was taken to the Egyptian Museum on the east bank.

The fragments of papyri which ended up in Paris, in the Museé du Louvre, had made a particularly remarkable journey. Although it sounds unbelievable and especially odd in view of the excited attention which they attracted from expert circles immediately on their discovery, they only came into the possession of the Louvre in 1956 and it is only from that year, more than half a century after their discovery, that serious research on the Abusir papyri began. It was also in 1952 that the librarian of the Bibliotheque de la Sorbonne, Louis Bonnerot, randomly opened a journal that had originally belonged to the celebrated French Egyptologist Gaston Maspero, a former director of the French Institute for Oriental Archaeology in Cairo. The journal was inherited by the library after Maspero's death. Two quite large fragments of papyri fell from the journal and thus came to the attention of Bonnerot. The distinguished Paris expert on papyri, Georges Posener, professor of Egyptology at the Sorbonne, identified them as part of the find made at the end of the previous century by the *sabbakhin* at Abusir. Only subsequently were the fragments transferred to the Museé du Louvre.

This time the interest excited in Parisian Egyptological circles by this small but historically significant discovery did not fade away. At Posener's instigation his student, later his wife, Paule Kriéger began to take a more systematic interest in the Abusir papyri. In 1956 she managed to find further papyrus fragments in the Louvre, in a folio deposited with other books of Maspero's in a trunk which had been transferred from the Bibliotheque de la Sorbonne four years before. From that moment, Paule Posener-Kriéger's career was to be inextricably linked with the fate of the Abusir papyri.

The attention attracted by the discovery of the Abusir papyri and their rapid plunge into obscurity was due to several factors. As has already been mentioned, the papyri consisted of fragments, altogether numbering a few hundred, and these fragments ranged in size from small pieces to major parts of entire scrolls. In the course of time, at the end of the 1930s and beginning of the 1940s, several small fragments had in fact been published by various scholars in connection with work on a number of subsidiary questions in Ancient Egyptian history.

For instance, after Selim Hassan's surprising discovery of the tomb of the Queen Khentkaus I in Giza, and the heated debate among scholars incited by the queen's unique title of the "Mother of Two kings of Upper and Lower Egypt" or "The King of Upper and Lower Egypt and Mother of the King of Upper and Lower Egypt," Borchardt decided to publish a fragment of papyrus which he had found in Neferirkare's mortuary temple which mentioned the "King's mother Khentkaus." It seemed to be logical to identify the queen Khentkaus from Giza with the king's mother Khentkaus mentioned on the fragment of papyrus from Abusir. At the time nobody knew that Neferirkare's consort was also named Khentkaus, and that her small pyramid complex lay only about 50 meters from the place where the papyrus fragment was found. Moreover, Borchardt's article led to the conclusion, widely accepted by scholarly public, that Neferirkare was a son of Khentkaus from Giza and one of the two kings mentioned in her unique title. The second king mentioned in the queen's title was identified as Sahure. This identification was made because of some additionally altered reliefs in Sahure's mortuary temple on which Kurt Sethe—a famous German Egyptologist who translated the inscriptions discovered by Borchardt in Sahure's pyramid complex—based his assumption that Neferirkare and Sahure were brothers. Though not supported by contemporaneous sources, the theory that Sahure and Neferirkare were sons of Khentkaus I then became established history.

However, let us return to the Abusir papyri. The first essential condition for scientific examination of the papyri was to order and classify them and to put together the parts that belonged to each other. This first step, apparently purely mechanical

A facsimile of the text with the name and title of the "King's mother Khentkaus." From the fragment of papyrus found in Neferirkare's mortuary temple.

Fragment of a relief from Sahure's mortuary temple. Shows a man in Sahure's entourage whose picture was subsequently altered into the pharaoh Neferirkare (by L. Borchardt).

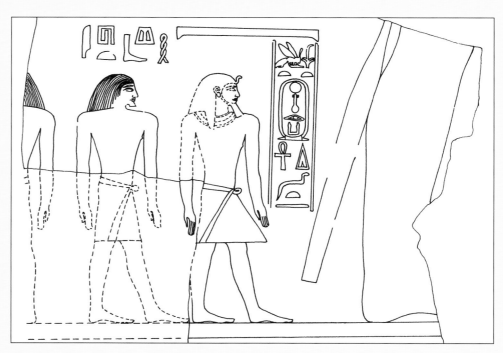

but in fact requiring long-term preparation and a basic grasp of the content of the individual fragments, was so difficult that at the beginning of the century nobody was willing to embark upon the task.

Another serious formal obstacle was represented by the texts themselves, and more precisely by the type of script used to make the records on the papyri. It was the early cursive type that today we call Old Hieratic. It was derived from hieroglyphic writing and used particularly on occasions when it was necessary to make a record quickly, simply and without ostentation, for example for the purposes of administration. The record was made with a small brush, most often in black but in special cases red and most frequently on a small sheet of papyrus but sometimes on a fragment of limestone, a shard of pottery, a wooden tablet or even an animal bone. It was a kind of writing that could turn into a scrawled line when the scribe was in a hurry, and this, of course, further complicates matters for the reader. The difficulties of reading Old Hieratic are increased still more by the fact that only a relatively limited number of examples exist. This means that the reader must have a thorough knowledge of the script and of the mechanism by which individual signs were simplified.

Additionally, the actual content of the hieratic records on the papyri in itself constituted a major obstacle. As at last became clear, they were records of very diverse kinds, from accounting documents on management of the temple cult to royal decrees. It is therefore no wonder that the Abusir papyri were only to "give utterance" three quarters of a century after they were found. When they did so it was thanks to the lifelong efforts of the late Paule Posener-Kriéger, formerly Director of the French Institute for Oriental Archaeology. Her efforts were supported by the encouragement and professional advice not only of Georges Posener but also of the British Egyptologist Sir Alan Gardiner—who even arranged for her a scholarship to edit the papyri—and, last but not least, by the Czech Egyptologist Jaroslav Černý, also a distinguished expert in hieratic paleography.

After more than twenty years of intensive work Paule Posener-Kriéger, in collaboration with the Museé du Louvre's long-time custodian Jean Louis de Cenival, published the set of papyri discovered in Neferirkare's pyramid temple and scattered in the aforementioned museums. The work, known as *The Abusir Papyri*, published in the form of an independent volume in the British Museum Series of Hieratic Texts in 1968, included a list of papyri, photocopies, hieroglyphic transcriptions of the hieratic texts, and relevant paleographical tables. Eight years later Mme. Posener-Kriéger added a translation and commentary. Under the title *Les archives du temple funéraire de Néferirkare-Kakaï* the two-volume work came out in 1976 in the Bibliotheque d'Études series published by the French Institute for Oriental Archaeology in Cairo. With these two volumes the richness of Neferirkare's temple archive was at last made accessible to the expert public.

The edition showed above all that the papyri represent only a fragment of the archive of Neferirkare's pyramid temple and that they are all in one way or another related to the pharaoh's mortuary cult. In several cases, the dating of the papyri has been made possible. As a matter of fact, on some of the papyri both the name of the king who issued the documents and the date referring to the year of the census of the country's wealth, the so-called cattle count, are present. Unfortunately, more precise dating of the documents is impossible because in the Old Kingdom the census took place irregularly, sometimes annually, sometimes biennially.

The papyri have thus been dated to a period between the concluding phase of the Fifth Dynasty and the end of the Sixth Dynasty, in other words, roughly to a period from the beginning of the twenty-fourth to the end of the twenty-third century BCE. The fact that a large proportion of the papyri have been identified as dating from the reign of Djedkare (only a smaller part of the papyri date from the reigns of Unas, Teti, and Pepi II) may be closely linked to the fact that it was this monarch who decided not to build his pyramid complex at Abusir, in the cemetery of his immediate royal predecessors, but several kilometers away in South Saqqara. Whatever Djedkare's reasons for building his tomb in another place were, the decision to abandon the Abusir necropolis obliged the king to undertake meticulous regulation both of the running of the mortuary cults in the individual pyramid complexes and of the general conditions in the necropolis. This is the background to which the large number of papyri dating from the time of Djedkare is related.

From the point of view of content, the papyri of Neferirkare's archive can be divided into several categories. Let us mention at least some of them.

One group is represented by rosters of priestly duties in Neferirkare's pyramid temple. These were tasks carried out daily in the morning and in the evening, monthly, or on the occasion of important festivals. They consisted of bringing offerings to the spirit of the deceased, sacrificial rites, and guard duties in various parts of the mortuary temple, among other activities. Particular services would be undertaken on the occasion of religious festivals such as the festival of Sokar (on the twenty-sixth day of the fourth month of the inundation season), during which this god of the dead visited the Abusir valley temples in his barque and was received there by the dead kings. Another festival, that of the Night of Re, undoubtedly preceded the feast of Re and probably took place in Neferirkare's sun temple on New Year's Day—although we do not know whether this was on the lunar or civic New Year's Day. The festival of the goddess Hathor was cele-

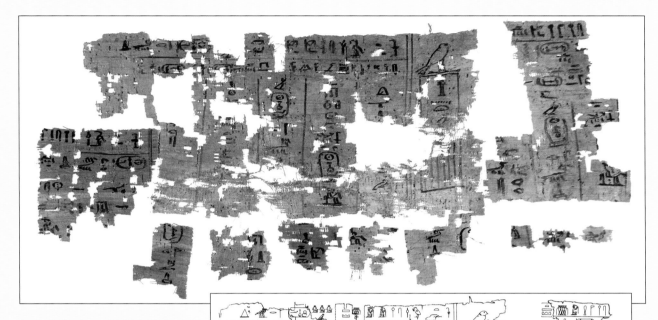

brated both in Neferirkare's mortuary and sun temples during the inundation.

According to the papyri, the priesthood in the mortuary temple was made up of the "servants of god (prophets)," "the pure," and the *khentyu-sh*, "the tenants" (the translation and interpretation of this Egyptian name is still the subject of academic debate). Various officials and workers and others would help them in the performance of their duties. The priesthood was divided into five basic groups, the so-called *phylai*—designated in terms of the parts of a boat, for example "prow—starboard," "stern—port,"— which were subdivided further into sections. Perhaps forty priests would make up one group. The lists suggest that the offices and professions represented among the priests and employees of the mortuary temple were extremely diverse; there were, for example, hairdressers, physicians, and scribes.

The inventory lists, which were a way of keeping track of the internal furnishings and equipment of the building, are very valuable in giving a better picture of the internal arrangement of the mortuary temple. Figuring in the lists are a whole range of different types of vessels, offering tables, ritual knives, materials, oils, jewelry, boxes, precious cult instruments, and incidental items. For each object there is a record, in a special column, indicating whether the object is or is not in its correct place, and whether it is damaged. Everything was recorded, from a wooden column in the temple courtyard damaged by fire to a broken pot. The bureaucratic thor-

Fragments of a decree issued by Djedkare. Neferefre's mortuary temple archive (photo: Kamil Voděra).

Hieroglyphic transcription of the hieratic text of a decree issued by Djedkare (by P. Posener-Kriéger).

oughness and precision of the priests and officials was so extreme that they did not hesitate to record that a small ball of incense was in its proper place in a box!

Accounting documents make up a large group of the papyri. Records concerning the supplies of various products and objects and their use or storage, documents pertaining to financial transactions and suchlike are only superficially dull. Deciphering them offers a unique key to understanding the complex mechanism by which the economic basis of the temple functioned. The wider economic context emerges here with unusual precision and sometimes brings surprises. They record yields from the estates specially allocated to provide material support to the pharaoh's mortuary cult; these included supplies of bread, cakes, beer, milk, wine, fruit, vegetables, fats, poultry, and meat. Naturally, they also mention other provisions such as cloth, staffs and maces, furniture, and much else.

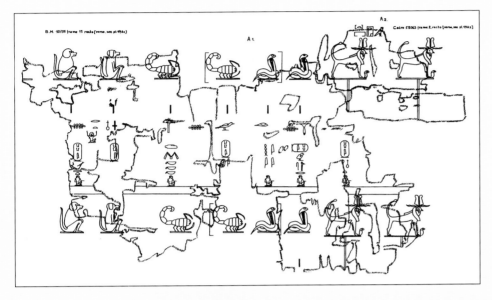

Fragment of papyrus from Neferirkare's mortuary temple archive with emblems of deities—a griffin, the cobra goddess Wadjet, the scorpion goddess Selket, and the baboon god Benet. The emblems, belonging to cult objects kept in the temple, were carried on the occasion of certain ceremonies that took place at the Abusir necropolis (by P. Posener-Kriéger).

Opposite:
Seated scribe writing on a papyrus scroll supported on his skirt, which is stretched tight between his knees. Polychrome limestone, 51 centimeters high. Egyptian Museum in Cairo (no. 36) (photo: Milan Zemina).

From the documents it is clear that supplies to the temple did not only flow in from the funerary estates that the king had set up during his lifetime to meet the needs of his mortuary cult. They also came from the stores of the royal residence, palace, and some other important central institutions. Among them, a special place was occupied by supplies from sun temples, especially Neferirkare's sun temple. These supplies had already been offered up on the altar of the sun god and only then were they taken to be offered on the altar of the deceased king in his pyramid temple. The sun temple of Neferirkare, though abundantly mentioned in the Abusir papyri, has, however, not yet been found, even though it was obviously located not far from Abusir.

Of the quite small group of surviving documents not yet mentioned, those directly related to the architecture of the pyramid complex have a special significance. These contain very heterogeneous and scrappy information connected, for example, with the regular sealing of doors in individual parts of the temple for purposes of inspection, the checking of possible damage to the temple's masonry, and other such matters. However fragmentary, this information acquires concrete archaeological importance when set side by side with the temple's real physical remains as uncovered during excavations. For example, in the papyri of Neferirkare's temple archive there is an allusion to damage being sustained to the masonry of the South Barque

during a service performed by one of the groups of priests. There is also an even more fragmentary mention of the North Barque. The assumption that two buildings—a South and a North Barque—had existed in the precincts of Neferirkare's pyramid complex became, at end of the 1970s, the starting-point for interesting archaeological research by the Czech team at Abusir. With the help of geophysical measuring, it proved possible to find and partially uncover the eastern half of a large, boat-shaped building in mud brick that had stood by the south wing of the enclosure wall of the pyramid, and precisely on its north–south axis. The building was originally about 30 meters long and contained a wooden boat in which the dead king could symbolically travel to the other world and join the entourage that accompanied the sun god on his eternal journey across the heavenly ocean. Unfortunately, all that has survived of the barque is moldering dust. The North Barque has not been uncovered, even though knowledge of the principles of Ancient Egyptian building suggests that it was extremely likely to have been situated— entirely symmetrically in relation to the South Barque—by the north enclosure wall of the pyramid.

By a curious coincidence, in 1976, the same year that Posener-Kriéger's book on the temple archives of Neferirkare was published, the Czech archaeological team in Abusir commenced excavation in a small pyramid complex situated about 50 meters south of Neferirkare's pyramid. Very soon, the complex proved to be the tomb of Neferirkare's consort Khentkaus II (for further details see Chapter IV). The monument was badly damaged by stone robbers who had quarried away large portions of the pyramid and most of a small limestone temple at the foot of the pyramid's east wall. In the debris filling the open pillared courtyard of the temple other fragments of papyri were found. At first sight, the papyri seemed to be of the same kind as those found just a few meters away, in the southwest storerooms of Neferirkare's mortuary temple. The remnants of a small wooden chest were found close to the papyri in which the latter may originally have been kept.

The papyri from Khentkaus II's temple represent the second papyrus archive found in Abusir. It consisted of about one hundred fragments, most of them very

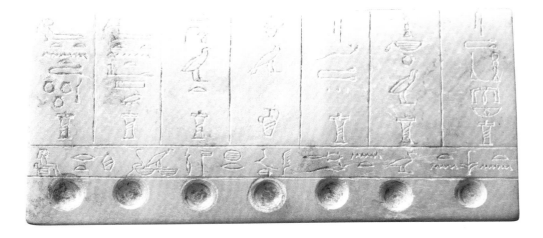

Alabaster tablet of "the seven offering oils" found in the mastaba of Khekeretnebty at Abusir (photo: Milan Zemina).

small. Only a few pieces were as large as a human palm. These papyri, too, were examined by Posener-Kriéger, and published by her in our joint volume *The Pyramid Complex of Khentkaus*. Today the papyri are in the Egyptian museum in Cairo.

Though the name of the royal mother Khentkaus does not occur on any of the fragments, the texts that survived leave no doubt that they made up part of the queen's temple archive. On five fragments there is a representation of a female figure standing in a shrine, wearing a vulture head-dress and holding in her hand a *was*-scepter. Since no specific attributes of a divinity accompany the figures on the fragments, this image most probably represented the owner of the mortuary temple herself, Khentkaus II. Moreover, the fragments of texts seem to indicate, quite strongly, that the pictures represent Khentkaus's cult statues. Thanks to the detailed description of materials from which the statues were made, we learn that the *naos* was of wood and decorated with lapis lazuli, the queen's necklace was of gold, the eyes were inlayed with onyx, the *was*-scepter was made of electrum, and so on. The papyri also indicate that in the mortuary temple there were originally at least sixteen cult statues of the royal mother. Regardless of all these details, the kind of the document from which the fragments come remains rather obscure. They may have originally come from a sort of an inventory of the temple cult objects.

If Neferirkare's temple archive had remained shrouded in mystery and the precise archaeological circumstances of the discovery remained unknown, then the third papyrus archive of Abusir, found in Neferefre's mortuary temple, was in this respect the complete reverse. It was possible to record carefully every detail of the archaeological context in which these papyri were discovered and, consequently, to bring together a mass of important supplementary information. Major assistance with unearthing and documentation of the papyri was provided to the Czech expedition by the late Paule Posener-Kriéger. By a lucky coincidence, shortly before the discovery of the papyri in Neferefre's mortuary temple, she had been appointed the

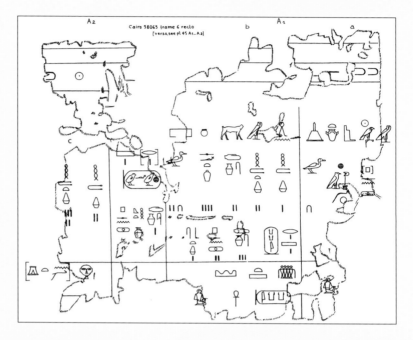

The text on a fragment of papyrus from Neferirkare's mortuary temple mentions, among other things, deliveries coming from the king's sun temple (by P. Posener-Kriéger).

director of the French Institute for Oriental Archaeology in Cairo. Our joint efforts were successful and over 2000 fragments, including entire large sections of papyrus scrolls, were retrieved, documented and provisionally lodged in the storage facility of the Czech expedition at Abusir. Because of security reasons, the papyri were moved to the Egyptian museum in Cairo before the end of the season.

The papyri were found in several different places of Neferefre's mortuary temple. The largest number were found in the storage rooms in the northwest part of the temple. There were so many there that their fragments had created an almost continuous layer on the floor of three of the storage rooms. The papyrus scrolls had originally been fastened with leather straps and lodged in wooden boxes. It is probable that later, when the temple was ransacked, thieves regarded the ornamented boxes as valuable but ignored the papyri. The contents of the boxes were tipped out onto the ground and, in the course of time, the papyri were trampled underfoot, submerged in rubbish and covered over by layers of crumbled, collapsing brick masonry from the rooms. Finally, everything was engulfed by vast layers of sand which safely preserved the remains of the papyri for four and a half millennia.

Facsimile of the remnants of the picture of Khentkaus II's statue standing in a naos. From a fragment of papyrus found in the mortuary temple of the queen.

It is almost unbelievable that these papyri, fragile as a spider's web, have survived to this day. Originally, of course, they were elastic and robust. This was a consequence both of the material—the pulp of the papyrus stems—and the technology for producing the scrolls. They were made by laying narrow strips cut from papyrus pulp crosswise over each other. No glue was used to stick the strips together since the papyrus juice, squeezed out from the pulp under the pressure of a stone press and then gradually dried out, was sufficient to bind the strips together.

The scribe's activities—both the method of writing and the writing materials used—in no way damaged the structure of the papyrus. The records were made with a small brush prepared from a thin reed stem, the end softened by chewing and formed into a tip. The scribe dipped the brush either into black ink (made of soot diluted with water) or into a red ink prepared from powdered ochre, likewise mixed with water. This meant that, when necessary, the text could be removed with water. The scroll could then be used again for making another record. A whole range of such re-used papyri, known as palimpsests, was found among the fragments from Neferefre's archive. Of course, if a papyrus scroll was exposed to the action of water for a longer time, or was left in damp conditions, it would be entirely destroyed.

In the case of Neferefre's temple archive a number of fortunate accidents occurred and these contributed to the preservation of the papyri, albeit in a fragmentary state. The first of these was the layer of dust and rubbish that had already covered the fragments at the time when the rooms in which the papyri lay were still roofed and were therefore still watertight. Another happy accident was that the brick masonry of the rooms progressively disintegrated and gradually settled on the layer of rubbish covering the papyri. In the end, this layer was so thick that it was not damaged by the collapse of the side walls, with their larger volume and weight, as a result of erosion. The huge layer of sand blown onto the ruins of the temple by the desert wind also proved ultimately beneficial, because it hid the papyri and the ruins from sight.

In overall volume, Neferefre's archive is comparable to that of Neferirkare.

Experienced workmen carefully uncovering and lifting fragments of the papyrus archive of Neferefre's mortuary temple (photo: Josef Grabmüller).

The major part of the papyrus archive was found in three magazines in the furthest northwest corner of Neferefre's mortuary temple (photo: Kamil Voděra).

Though with certain divergences, the basic content of the surviving documents is also similar. For example, a higher number of royal decrees, often regulating the economic conditions of certain categories of the temple priesthood, have been preserved in Neferefre's archive. Most of these decrees, if not all of them, seem to have been issued by Djedkare.

Surprisingly, a relatively high number of documents with dates has survived, more than in Neferirkare's temple archive. Most of them seem to refer to Djedkare's reign, some of them possibly to the time of Unas, too.

Of course, among the papyri one can also find documents with rosters concerning the service in Neferefre's mortuary temple. They contain detailed information on the organization of the temple priesthood, schedules for the service of different *phylai* in the temple, lists of responsible officials, and so on. A variety of personal names and titles, many of them intimately known to us already from Neferirkare's temple archive, are mentioned in these papyri. Of special importance are the names of officials whose tombs have already been identified and unearthed in Abusir. Concerning the titles, perhaps one of the most curious temple professions documented in Neferefre's temple archive was undoubtedly the "flute-player of the White Crown"—a man who played the flute during the ceremony connected with venerating the crown that symbolically made the pharaoh the ruler of Upper Egypt.

As in Neferirkare's temple archive, accounting documents form a large portion of the papyri found in Neferefre's temple. They inform us in detail about the supplies coming to the temple from the funerary estates, the royal residence, the temple of Ptah and, most significantly, from Neferirkare's sun temple. As a matter of fact,

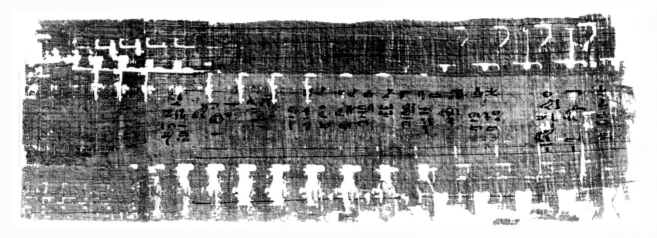

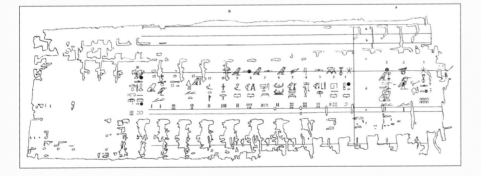

Incomplete scroll of papyrus from Neferefre's temple archive with a list of cult objects. Among the objects kept in the temple were wooden statues of a heron and a hippopotamus (photo: Milan Zemina).

Hieroglyphic transcription of the hieratic text regarding the cult objects kept in Neferefre's mortuary temple (by P. Posener-Kriéger).

Neferefre's sun temple was, at the moment of the king's untimely death, only just begun, and was never finished. Some of these accounting documents are especially interesting and important.

Inventory lists represent another group of papyri in Neferefre's archive. These documents, which mostly relate to regular revisions, help us to get a better idea of the temple's inventory, which included a variety of objects from cult statues to different instruments used in the temple rituals. Thanks to one of these lists we know that in the Neferefre's temple inventory there were, for example, wooden statues of a heron and a hippopotamus.

Eventually, a brief mention at least should be made of one very significant archaeological aspect of the papyri found to date in Abusir. Some of the documents explicitly mention edifices which must have once existed in the Abusir necropolis and which have not yet been identified. For instance, the "Southern sanctuary," the palace named "Sahure's-splendor-soars-to-the-sky," and others. It is not necessary to emphasize what a great archaeological challenge these documents provide for Egyptological scholars today.

What remains to be said? We should perhaps express regret that other papyrus archives are unlikely to be discovered at Abusir. The discovery of the remnants of three temple archives—those of Neferirkare, Neferefre and Khentkaus—has been to some extent a matter of chance and the coincidence of a few unique historical circumstances. Under normal conditions the analogous papyrus archives of the royal pyramid complexes were not kept in the storerooms of the mortuary temples, but in the administrative buildings, which, together with the priests' dwellings, were concentrated in the immediate vicinity of the valley temples, i.e. in the so-called pyramid towns. In other words, they were kept not in the tomb complex but still in the "world of the living," although in close proximity to the entry to the "realm of the dead." At

Abusir such towns, in which priests, officials and workmen employed in the mortuary cults at the cemetery lived and worked, almost certainly existed in the vicinity of Sahure's and Niuserre's valley temples. Their remains lie today perhaps five meters beneath the surface of the desert, under great layers of Nile mud deposits. The current level of ground water in these places lies about one meter beneath the surface. This means that the papyrus archives in the administrative buildings of the pyramid towns have long disappeared without trace, dissolving and moldering into the mud that cradles them. It was only by sheer accident that Neferirkare did not finish his pyramid complex and that this was accomplished for him by his younger son, Niuserre, who then had the causeway leading from the valley to the mortuary temple of his father diverted and completed as a part of his own pyramid complex. The tombs of the older members of Niuserre's family, all by coincidence unfinished and only completed in his reign, were thus consigned to a somewhat autonomous and isolated position within the cemetery. For that reason their priests did

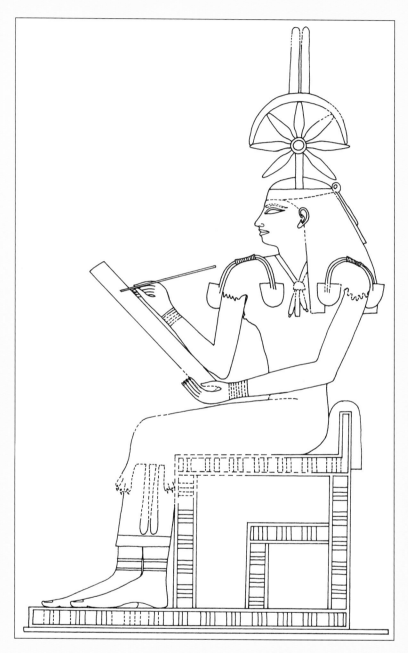

Seshat, the goddess of writing. Low relief from Sahure's mortuary temple at Abusir (by L. Borchardt).

not make their dwellings near valley temples on the edge of the desert, but in the immediate neighborhood of the mortuary chapels and gradually, even inside them. The higher site of the mortuary temples, perhaps 30 meters above the Nile Valley, and the hot and dry conditions of the desert had then only to interact favorably for the remains of the papyrus archives to be preserved to this day.

Head of a statue of the
Vizier Ptahshepses. The Vizier
wears a wig on his head and
a beard on his chin. Reddish
limestone, 23 centimeters high
(photo: Milan Zemina)

CHAPTER VII

The Dazzling Career of the Royal Hairdresser

ichard Lepsius, the celebrated founder of the first German department of Egyptology at Berlin University, and other members of the German expedition who visited Abusir in 1843, were convinced that the remains of a pyramid lay concealed under the huge ruins on the northeast edge of the necropolis. For this reason they assigned the Roman numeral XIX to this antiquity on the maps published subsequently in the first volume of their monumental work, *Denkmäler aus Aegypten und Aethiopien.* They had earlier decided to use Roman numerals to designate pyramids,

View of the mastaba of Ptahshepses from the top of Niuserre's pyramid
(photo: Kamil Voděra).

Builder's inscription revealed on a limestone block from the masonry of Ptahshepses' mastaba. The inscription dates from the "4th day of the 4th month of summer" and refers to "Khnumhotep," obviously an official responsible for the control of limestone blocks delivered to the building site of the mastaba (photo: Milan Zemina).

starting from the north and proceeding south. The number I was therefore assigned to a large mud brick building in Abu Rawash, perhaps seven kilometers north of Giza and regarded by the Lepsius expedition as the northernmost Egyptian pyramid. This was, by the way, a mistake because the mud brick ruin was not in fact a pyramid. As chance would have it, neither was "pyramid" no. XIX in Abusir. This was recognized by the French Egyptologist Jacques de Morgan, who started archaeological excavations in the ruins of the monument in 1893 and instead of a pyramid discovered the entrance to the mastaba of Ptahshepses.

The entrance to Ptahshepses' mastaba was decorated by a pair of eight-stem lotus columns of fine white limestone. These six-meter high columns represent the so far oldest known examples of their type from ancient Egypt (photo: Kamil Voděra).

The mastaba of Ptahshepses, of which de Morgan had uncovered only a small part, was then forgotten for almost seventy years. The revival of interest in the monument and completion of research into it was linked to the founding of the Czech (then Czechoslovak) Institute of Egyptology at Charles University and its branch in Cairo. The Institute acquired the concession permitting completion of the research on the mastaba of Ptahshepses in 1960 at the same time as it committed itself to take part in the UNESCO archaeological rescue operations in Nubia. The excavations in the mastaba of Ptahshepses were initiated in 1960 and up to the mid-1960s they were carried out in intervals between expeditions to Nubia. With the exception of the last season in 1974, they were led by Zbyněk Žába, with the valuable help of Abdu al-Qereti, the experienced foreman of the local workmen.

Excavations in the mastaba of Ptahshepses were undertaken over seven archaeological seasons between 1960 and 1974. They

Reis Abdu al-Qereti directing the workmen at the excavation in the mastaba of Ptahshepses (photo: Milan Zemina).

resulted in the unearthing of what is as yet the most extensive and architecturally the most complex non-royal tomb known from the period of the Old Kingdom. In fact, many features incorporated into the design of the Ptahshepses mastaba were more or less inspired by royal architecture. The tomb had been constructed in three major building phases, in other words, its design was been modified twice in the interests of creating a larger and architecturally more demanding structure. What ultimately emerged was a building that had no parallel in its time. Viewed from the Nile Valley, the mastaba of Ptahshepses once stood majestically on the edge of the raised desert plateau, alongside the pyramids of the kings its owner had served. The smooth, rectangular, white limestone walls of the mastaba would have shone brightly in the intense rays of the sun and would have harmoniously complemented the similarly shining immense triangular surfaces of the neighboring pyramids. The site for Ptahshepses' mastaba was not chosen at random. On the contrary, the site in front of the pyramids of Sahure and Niuserre, and almost precisely equidistant from both, was chosen very deliberately. It was as if the owner and builder of the mastaba had

Following pages:
View of Ptahshepses' mastaba from the northeast (photo: Kamil Voděra).

wanted to round off the monumental architectonic composition of all the tombs of the kings and magnates of which he had himself been to a considerable extent the designer. From Ptahshepses' titles it is clear that he was overseer of all the royal building works in the land.

The entrance to the tomb, situated in the eastern wall near the northeast corner, was adorned with a pair of six-meter-high eight-stemmed columns shaped like lotus sheaves with closed buds and tied under the capitals with cord wound several times around them. Each column was made from a single piece of the fine white limestone which Arabs today call *batn al-baqara*, ("Cow's Belly"), perhaps because this is what the color and smoothness of the stone brings to mind. The columns supported a heavy architrave on which rested the enormous slabs of the roof terrace. Both architrave and slabs were of the same high-quality limestone as the columns. Originally the portico reached a height of eight meters. The eight-stemmed lotus columns are, at present, the oldest known examples of their type from Ancient Egypt. It is no accident that this unique example of the technical imagination of the Ancient Egyptians first appears in Abusir and here in the Mastaba of Ptahshepses: the eight stems geometrically and aesthetically allowed the most harmonious transition between the circular base on which the column stood and the square abacus on the lotus capital, on which again rested the rectangular architrave. Nor was the choice of plant motif, that

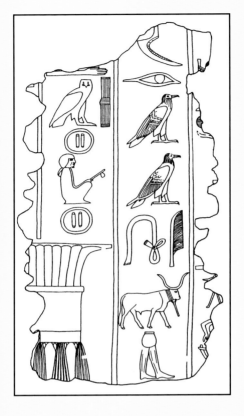

Fragment of a relief from Ptahshepses' mastaba with the remains of a text, and a part of the portico which formed the architrave decorated with a concave cornice and supported by an eight-stem lotus column.

Plan of Ptahshepses's mastaba, which indicates the three building phases of the monument (by P. Jánosi).

The young sons of Ptashepses carrying hoopoes. One of them is holding his father's staff, another is sniffing at a lotus flower. Low relief with remains of polychrome. Mastaba of Ptahshepses, Abusir.

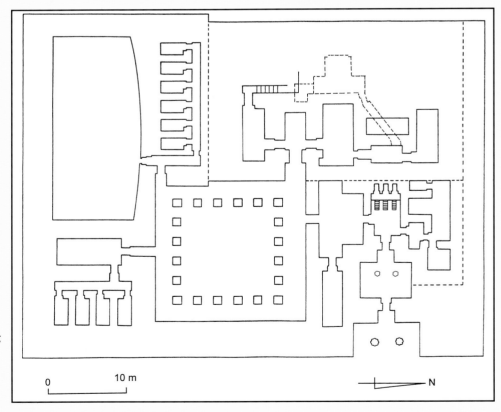

0   10 m

N

Previous pages:
Detail of a man
pouring water
across the deck of
a boat. Low relief
with remains
of polychrome.
Mastaba of
Ptahshepses,
Abusir (photo:
Milan Zemina).

of the lotus, a matter of chance. The lotus, whose flower closes at night and sinks into the water and then at morning opens again, was a symbol of resurrection and rebirth in Ancient Egypt. This was not really a columned entrance to a tomb; it was rather the gateway to resurrection and a new life, eternal and blissful.

Lotus columns, but this time only six-stemmed, also adorned the room onto which the monumental entrance opened. This columned vestibule was, in the second stage of building, planned to be the main entrance, but it lost its function during the third stage, becoming a closed room. Its walls are decorated with scenes of boats and bearers bringing from the funerary estates and workshops Ptahshepses's burial equipment and everything else necessary for setting up the mortuary cult: furniture, jewellery, cloth, grain, fruit, and the like. Near the entrance to the vestibule the torso

of a large seated statue of Ptahshepses was found. Probably what is known as the 'biographical inscription' was first placed in this columned vestibule, too. It is a great pity that only a few fragments of this inscription have been found, for its loss means that Ptahshepses' origins and the circumstances of his dizzying social ascent remain shrouded in mystery.

Scenes of the slaughter of sacrificial animals and pictures of Ptahshepses fill up the walls of a narrow passage leading from the columned vestibule to one of the most important cult rooms in the tomb— the chapel with the three niches. Inscriptions accompanying the pictures contain a range of titles which attest to Ptahshepses' high social status: "Local

The Vizier
Ptahshepses
with his wife,
the princess
Khamerernebty,
kneeling at his
feet. Detail
from the relief
decoration of
Ptahshepses'
mastaba.

Prince, Only Friend (of the pharaoh), Ruler of Nekheb, Guardian of the (royal) Diadem, Privy to the Secret of the House of Morning, Beloved One of his Lord, Chief Justice, Vizier, Overseer of all the Royal Works, Servant of the Throne, Lector-Priest, Privy to the Secret Sacred Writings of the God's Words . . ."

The chapel with the three niches in its western wall had an important cult function. Originally, slightly larger than life-size statues of the standing Ptahshepses, made out of reddish quartzite, stood in these niches behind narrow two-leaf doors. Only fragments of these statues were found. Judging from the inscriptions on the facing wall of the niches, the statues represented Ptahshepses in three different forms or functions: as an official, as a priest, and as a private individual. Offerings were placed on altars at the foot of the statues during funerary ceremonies accompanied by the recitation of religious formulae spoken by the lector-priest: The scenes on the walls then revived and created the intimate world of the blissful eternity enjoyed by the deceased in the other world.

The greater part of the low polychrome relief decorating the chapel walls has survived to this day. The scenes depicted here are thematically linked by a single basic idea: the owner of the tomb overseeing work in his fields, pastures, gardens, and workshops, where all that is necessary for his mortuary cult is grown, manufactured and collected. On the chapel's northern wall there are scenes in which gardeners are working in the fields of grain and vegetable plots, while bearers, entrusted with carrying the fruits of the fields and gardens are bringing them on offering tables and in baskets to the feet of Ptahshepses. On the south wall there are fishermen, herdsmen milking cows, and the overseer of a poultry farm driving flocks of duck, geese, and

Detail from a scene of the bringing of offering gifts. Low relief with remains of polychrome. Mastaba of Ptahshepses, Abusir (photo: Milan Zemina).

cranes in front of him. And there are also, of course, scribes who are carefully record-
ing everything on papyrus scrolls.

On the northern part of the east wall of the chapel there are superb scenes of a
sculptor's atelier where two of Ptahshepses' statues—one in red granite and seated
and the other in wood and standing—are being finished. Metal founders and chis-
ellers are also depicted at their work, together with carpenters making a staff.

Opposite the scenes of crafts and near the entrance from the columned vestibule is
an apparently simple but in fact very curious scene depicting the six sons of
Ptahshepses walking. The figure and name of the first-born have been carefully chis-
eled off and almost entirely removed. Two of the sons bore the same name as their
father, Ptahshepses, the others being called Kahotep, Hemakhty, and Khenu. With
appropriate lighting it also proved possible to decipher the name of the first-born
son—Khafini. The form of this name is of no small significance for the reconstruction
of the chronology both of the tomb and of Ptahshepses' family relationships. This is
because the name Khafini is basiloform, containing *Ini*—one of the names of the king
Niuserre—in a cartouche. This name also represents an important date indicating *post
quem* that Ptahshepses was approximately Niuserre's contemporary. The chiseling off
of the name—and there is a similar example elsewhere in the tomb—points to a deliberate action which, according to the religious ideas of the Ancient Egyptians, would
have dire consequences. For them a name was one of the enduring spiritual elements
of a person and lasted beyond his earthly lifetime. The explanation for the action perhaps lay in family disputes triggered by Ptahshepses' marriage to the pharaoh
Niuserre's daughter Khamererrnebty. Ptahshepses, a man of non-royal origin, gained
this extraordinary honor only at an advanced age, when he was already at the peak of
his official career. It is almost unimaginable that at that time he would not already have
had a family for many years and that this family would have had to give place to the
new family, immediately related to the pharaoh. It was perhaps for this reason that the
first-born son of the non-royal family had to yield to the first-born in whose veins ran
royal blood. The ramifications of these events can only be guessed at.

In the northern part of the mastaba, there were four rooms that once served as
magazines for offerings and cult vessels for ceremonies carried out in the neighboring large chapel with three niches.

On the wall of the eastern part of the "southern portico," opening the way from
the chapel with three niches to the pillared courtyard, Ptahshepses is depicted surrounded by his subordinate officials. On the northern wall of the "southern portico" he is being carried on a litter for a walk. An interesting inscription has survived
above the line of men carrying Ptahshepses. It contains a dialogue between the first
and the last, the man leading and supervising and the man at the end of the row of

bearers. The bearer at the rear is being reprimanded and asked to calm down and fulfill his bearer's duties well. But the subject of the reprimand is holding his ground and sarcastically commenting that the chief, called the "privileged one," would do better to mind his own business and follow his nose. From this sneering remark it is apparent that the man selected as the leader and supervisor of the bearers was probably one of them and enjoyed no great respect among his fellows.

The western part of the "southern portico" is decorated with scenes depicting the transport of Ptahshepses' statues and of the storage of the offerings. The striding statues were dragged in a way characteristic of Ancient Egyptians, on wooden sleds over a pre-leveled route, which, during transport, would also be smoothed with water mixed with soft Nile mud. This would create a slippery surface making transport easier. From the inscriptions accompanying these scenes it is clear that some of the statues were of red granite and measured seven cubits, or approximately three and a half meters height. Is this an allusion to the magical number "7"? Or, were there really colossal statues of Ptahshepses in his mastaba? So far, the scarce evidence from the Old Kingdom suggests that colossal statues were likely to be only royal privileges. Though during excavations in the mastaba a large number of fragments of alabaster, red granite, limestone, and red

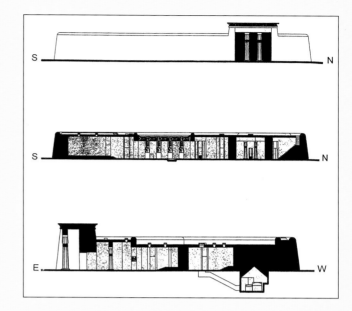

Ptahshepses' mastaba (from above downwards). View of the eastern facade, north–south cross-section of the eastern half of the mastaba and the east-west section of the northern half of the mastaba (by M. Balík).

A scene of men dragging a pair of Ptahshepses' striding statues in red granite on a wooden sledge. The statues are placed in a naos. Western wall of the portico linking the three niched chapel with the pillared courtyard. Ptahshepses' mastaba.

quartzite, which came from several dozen statues were discovered, none of them comes from a colossal statue of Ptahshepses. Be that as it may, the question of where all these statues—mostly of Ptahshepses and his consort Khamerernebty—had been positioned in the tomb and what cult function they fulfilled is complex and has still not been satisfactorily answered.

The pillared court came into existence only with the third, concluding building phase of the mastaba. The disintegrated crowns of twenty monolithic limestone pillars were measured and marked on a plan by de Morgan, but the pillared court was, as a whole, uninvestigated. West of the pillared court, de Morgan uncovered the entrance to what seemed to be another mastaba. Given the very limited extent of his excavations it is not surprising that he judged it to belong to a tomb quite other than that of Ptahshepses. He even believed that a whole group of mastabas were to be found on the site. It was only with Žába excavation that it became clear that what was being partly revealed by de Morgan was not another tomb, but Ptahshepses's "original mastaba," constructed during the first building stage of his funerary monument.

Originally, offerings were made in the pillared courtyard under the open sky on a huge altar, the upper face of which was decorated with the large hieroglyphic sign *hetep* meaning "offering" or "offering table." The side walls of the courtyard were once richly decorated with reliefs, of which only a tiny fragment has survived *in situ*. The flat roof of limestone slabs that protected the reliefs was supported by twenty monolithic (made, in other words, from a single block of stone) pillars. The faces of the pillars that were turned inward to the court bore life-size pictures of Ptahshepses in sunk relief. The figures of Ptahshepses were arranged on the pillars in such a way as to lead the visitor from the south, on a north–south axis, into the courtyard and in the direction of the altar, thence to the northwestern corner of the courtyard towards the entrance to the "original mastaba," and thus towards Ptahshepses' burial chamber. Above the figures and likewise in sunk relief—a type of relief particularly suitable for open space accessible to sunlight because it allows the aesthetic effect of pictures and inscriptions to be deepened by the play of light and shadow—Ptahshepses' titles and name were carved. None of the crowns of the pillars have been preserved in their entirety and they have all been damaged by natural erosion. Nonetheless, some of their fragments have survived. It is clear from the inscriptions on several of these fragments that Ptahshepses's titulary began with the title "King's Son." At the time that the final extension of the mastaba was underway, then, Ptahshepses had already become a prince, undoubtedly as a result of his marriage to Khamerernebty, daughter of the pharaoh Niuserre. At that time, it was exceptional that a private person should not only become a member of the immediate royal family but also should be allowed to use a royal title, the title of prince. Ptahshepses had reached the height of

Pillar with picture of the magnate Ptashepses in sunk relief. Mastaba of Ptashepses, Abusir (photo: Milan Zemina).

Following pages: Abusir. View of the pillared courtyard of Ptahshepses' mastaba from the northeast. In the background the pyramid of Niuserre can be seen (photo: Kamil Voděra).

his dazzling career: the royal hairdresser and manicurist had become the king's son. It is, of course, necessary to bear in mind that a royal hairdresser and manicurist was not so lowly a personage as it might seem today. The fact that in the course of his duties he was allowed to touch the body of the one god living among men on earth, the pharaoh, gained him, to a certain extent for religious reasons, an important status and thus would have smoothed his path to other still higher offices at the royal court.

Two large magazine complexes, one comprising four chambers to the southeast of the pillared courtyard and the other seven chambers to the southwest, both uncovered in the second half of the 1960s, only strengthen the overall impression of a half-private, half-royal tomb. Magazine complexes similar to those found in the mastaba—the so-called treasury and granary—are to be found particularly in contemporary royal pyramid temples.

If these features which were incorporated into the design of Ptahshepses's mastaba were more or less inspired by royal architecture, then a room in the southwest corner of the tomb was a completely unexpected surprise for the excavators and also left no one in doubt of the extraordinarily high and truly exceptional social standing of the tomb's owner. This room is the largest in the tomb and in shape resembles a boat. Its northern wall is not only convex but curved in a way that visibly recalls the side of a boat. We meet with the burial of boats, from this period, above all in royal pyramid complexes, because the boat journey in the other world in the entourage of the sun god was exclusively a royal privilege. The famous Barque of Khufu, discovered by the Egyptian archaeologists in 1954 near the south side of the Great Pyramid at Giza and today exhibited in its own "Museum of the Boat of Cheops" close to the site of the find, is an outstanding embodiment of this religious idea. . Did Ptahshepses also endeavour to share the royal privilege? Eventually, however, the room—large enough to accomodate a pair of boats—was left unfinished.

The "original mastaba" in the northwest part of Ptahshepses's funerary monument represents the earliest building stage of the tomb. It was once a complete tomb with slightly inclined walls built of white limestone slabs. In the area of this "original mastaba" a large number of relief fragments were found. These were not, however, from Ptahshepses's mastaba. The fragments had been stored, or more precisely, left to one side, here by Borchardt in the course of his excavations in Sahure's neighboring pyramid temple. The great majority of these fragments had never been published by Borchardt. A rusty tin, a scrap of a German newspaper and an envelope stamped "January 1904," accompanied and dated Borchardt's deposit. Unfortunately, of the once rich relief decoration and many inscriptions which decorated the walls of the "original mastaba" only two fragments have been preserved *in situ*: a few square centimeters showing the lower part of the figure of an offering bearer and, on the eastern wall of the *serdab*, a much larger fragment of the lower part of a finely carved, polychromed false door imitating the facade of a royal palace. In the floor under the false door there was a shaft giving access to Ptahshepses's burial chamber.

It is both remarkable and mysterious that the burial chamber, even in the original mastaba, had already been constructed on the model of royal burial chambers, with a gabled ceiling built of huge monolithic limestone blocks. Two nicely executed red

View into the burial chamber of the mastaba of Ptahshepses. The larger sarcophagus, made of Aswan red granite, belonged to Ptahshepses and the smaller, made of the same material, very probably to his wife, the princess Khamerernebty (photo: Milan Zemina).

granite sarcophagi, unfortunately robbed in antiquity, were found in this burial chamber—the larger, very well preserved, for Ptahshpepses and the smaller, with its lid broken in pieces, for Khamerernebty. The princess's sarcophagus, however, could not possibly have been transported there by way of the narrow descending passage. In the original plan of the chamber only Ptahshepses' sarcophagus had been taken into account. In any case, Khamerernebty had an already completed burial chamber of her own in the neighboring Mastaba of the Princesses, discovered by Borchardt near the northeast corner of Niuserre's pyramid temple. The terms of the original plan of Ptahshepses's mastaba were therefore disregarded; Khamerernebty's sarcophagus was placed in Ptahshepses' burial chamber, although this must have happened at a time when the original mastaba was still only half-built so the burial chamber was still open and Khamerernebty's sarcophagus could thus still be lowered into it from above. In this context it is not insignificant that the name of Princess Khamerernebty has been found among the inscriptions recorded by the builders in red directly on the rough limestone blocks that were used to construct the core of the original mastaba.

All this evidence indicates that Princess Khamerernebty apparently began to play an ever more significant role in the life of Ptahshepses (or he in hers) relatively soon after the start of work on the building of the original mastaba. Unfortunately, we cannot reconstruct the very beginning of Ptahshepses's career from the almost totally destroyed reliefs in the original mastaba, and the few fragments which survived from the previously mentioned biographical inscription of Ptahshepses. The builders' inscriptions, however, enable us to date the beginning of the construction of Ptahshepses's original mastaba to the time shortly before the tenth regnal year of Niuserre and its conclusion to the time about the thirtieth regnal year of the king. What could have been happening then at the royal court, inside the royal family and at the top of the country's pyramid of power if the royal hairdresser and high official could begin to concentrate power and wealth in his own hands which was eventually so great that he could be on an equal footing with those who were the direct issue of the pharaoh, the living god on earth? We can only guess at the answer, and put it together from the fragments of information that have gradually been found during archaeological excavations at other places in the Abusir necropolis, for example at the so-called Unfinished Pyramid (see above, Chapter V).

Like the royal pyramids and rich tombs which surround it, the exquisite mastaba of Ptashepses was ravaged by looters, probably during the First Intermediate Period. Ptahshepses' mummy was destroyed as well. This, according to Ancient Egyptian conceptions, was the most terrible fate that might befall a person. The soul of Ptahshepses could no longer visit his body and his image, and could no longer receive offerings and live "forever in eternity." One of the fundamental aims behind Ptashepses' striving and vertiginous ascent—the longing to build, in his tomb, a "palace of the spirit" which would endure through the ages—would, in the end, be frustrated. Of the magnates and those nearly equal to the pharaoh there have remained only a few fragments of bone, and of the once undoubtedly rich funerary equipment in his tomb, only a few insignificant scraps. The abandoned mastaba of Ptahshepses, gradually disintegrating and vanishing under the sand dunes, defied this merciless fate for several centuries. Under the New Kingdom, in the Nineteenth Dynasty and in the reign of Ramsesses the Great and his successors, it was, like many other burial monuments in the area, gradually dismantled and some of its parts were re-used for the construction of other buildings. At this period a stone-masonry workshop was set up inside the mastaba, and here the stone broken away from its walls was prepared as if in a quarry. Nomads even camped with their herds of goats and sheep in the Boat Hall. This work of destruction then continued in intervals up to the Roman era and, in the end, the ruins vanished under a six-meter layer of sand and rubble.

Ptahshepses' "double-portrait." The sculptor who carved the figure of the tomb's owner in low relief in the chapel with the three niches wrongly estimated the space for the figure and then had to correct his error (photo: Milan Zemina).

CHAPTER VIII

The Traitor's Tomb?

T he Memphite necropolis has been a center of archaeological interest from as early as the start of the last century. It has been criss-crossed by the paths of many scientific expeditions and archaeological surveys. Major reconstruction projects are constantly underway here. The mass of published information and the detailed archaeological maps of individual localities suggest, at first sight, that everything here has long ago been discovered, and studied and described several times over. The casual observer might easily believe that there is now no scope left for a new and surprising archaeological find. But this would be a very superficial and inaccurate impression. On the archaeological map of the necropolis there are "white" areas: places about which we know little or nothing. These are, in fact, extensive, and they exist at Abusir as well. One could almost say that they represent the greater part of this particular royal necropolis. The Abusir cemetery was not, after all, composed only of pyramids and the tombs lying in their immediate neighborhood.

Until recently, Egyptologists and archaeologists looked at Abusir in a distinctly one-sided way. Thanks to the pyramids that the pharaohs of the Fifth Dynasty built here, Abusir was considered to be a royal cemetery belonging exclusively to that period. Moreover, the belief prevailed that all that was historically significant and interesting here had already been discovered and studied, particularly during the German Oriental Society's expedition at the beginning of the last century. In recent years there has been a widespread change in this regard and one of the major reasons has been the surprising discovery of a cemetery with shaft tombs dating from the end of the Twenty-sixth and the beginning of the Twenty-seventh Dynasty, in other words from

On the way to the Abusir necropolis (photo Kamil Voděra).

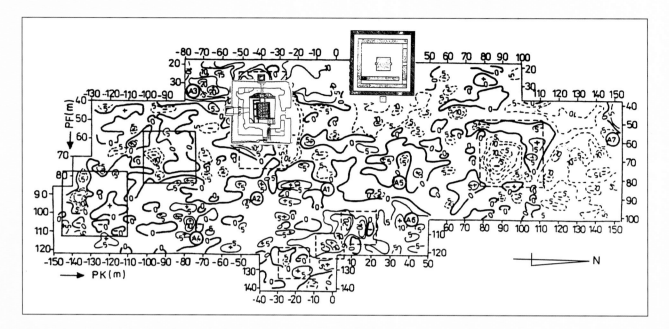

A map drawn on the basis of geophysical measuring in the southwest sector of the Abusir cemetery shows the approximate location of the shaft tombs from the Saite-Persian period (by V. Hašek).

the end of what is known as the Saite Period and the beginning of Persian Domination over Egypt. Deep in the desert almost one kilometer west of the edge of the Nile Valley, in an area already apparently far back from the Abusir pyramid field, a group of large square-shaped structures was found at the end of the 1970s and beginning of the 1980s. It was found partly as a result of a hint on an old map of Abusir drawn up in 1843 by the Lepsius expedition but mostly through the extensive geophysical survey carried out by the Czech Egyptological expedition. The survey indicated the existence of perhaps half a dozen large and several smaller structures, all square in ground plan, on an area of approximately half a square kilometer.

The excavations were initiated in 1980 and the first monument under investigation was allocated the identification mark "H" on the archaeological map of the Czech team at Abusir. The first days brought further puzzles rather than immediate explanations. What was found was a sizeable enclosure wall constructed of limestone blocks and defining a square area of ground measuring about 25.5 by 26 meters and containing flat irregular stones laid on a layer of sand, and the remains of mud brick structures. In the middle of this area was the mouth of a large shaft about five and a meters square above which rose the remains of a false vault of limestone blocks (we can only speculate about the form of the structure which once surmounted the shaft: a small pyramid, a stylized primeval hill, or a small chapel?). It was only when the layer of sand and the stones, which had been laid without mortar, had been removed that the mouths of several long shafts were revealed and found to be arranged according to a very original plan. The large shaft, which has already been mentioned, was in the middle and on all four sides it was surrounded by shafts, rectangular in horizontal cross-section, which were arranged at regular intervals to form a square pattern.

Uncovering the intact foundation deposit, which was laid when work on commenced at the northwest corner of the stone enclosure wall of Udjahorresnet's shaft tomb at Abusir (photo: Milan Zemina).

Work on uncovering the site continued and brought further surprising discoveries: all the shafts had been filled up with very fine sand from which the coarser pebbles and small boulders had been removed by sieving. The peripheral shafts arranged in the square design were linked together at various levels by large apertures such that the fine sand could flow freely through them. The bottom of the peripheral shafts had still not been reached when excavation work in them was stopped in several places at a depth of approximately 15 meters and sounding probes using a strong steel rod were used to find out how much further they descended. This measure was dictated by the fact that further excavation of the shafts could have endangered the stability of the whole tomb complex. This was because the system of shafts had not been dug in a homogeneous rock base but in a thick layer of the hardened marl clay, in Arabic called *tafla*, interwoven with narrow layers of petrified salt. The probes indicated that the shafts continued down to a depth of at least 20 meters. At the bottom of the central shaft, however, at a depth of about 14 meters, the vaulted ceiling of the burial chamber was discovered.

A winch is indispensable for work in shaft tombs (photo: Milan Zemina).

The chamber, including the ceiling, had been constructed of well crafted blocks of fine white limestone. Thieves had once tunneled a hole in the massive vaulted ceiling. When they broke into the burial chamber they too must have had to clear away the sand filling of the shaft from the greater part of it. This route was clearly not the original access route to the burial chamber. This had been by a smaller, so-called 'side shaft' discovered in front of the eastern face of the stone enclosure wall of the tomb.

The central and side shafts, both located on the east–west axis of the tomb complex, were of roughly the same depth and were linked at the bottom by a short horizontal passage. This passage was not completely carved out of the clay base but was designed at one point to cross the eastern peripheral shaft, which had been placed like a "screen" between the side shaft and central shaft. The "screen" effect is apparent from the fact that the bottom of the eastern peripheral shaft is much lower than the floor of the horizontal passage that crosses it. The place where the shaft and the passage cut across each other represented the critical point of an entire security system. For this reason it was here that the tomb's architect installed a sophisticated drawbridge, or safety valve preventing entry to the burial chamber . He created it in the following way. He had the part of the horizontal passage that crossed the vertical eastern shaft constructed at the time when the shaft was already being filled with the fine sand. First, the limestone slabs

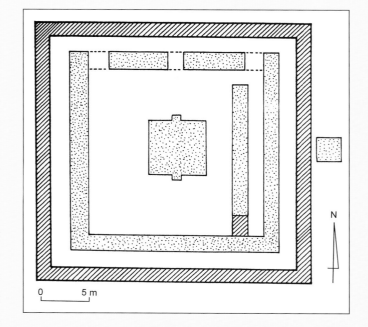

Horizontal cross-section at the foundation level of the superstructure of Udjahorresnet's shaft tomb. The plan shows the arrangement of shafts inside and outside the square stone enclosure wall of the tomb.

of paving were laid on the sand and then, likewise on the shaft's sand filling, the side walls of the perhaps two-meter section of the passage were constructed out of mud bricks. Finally an arch, also of mud brick and perhaps 70 cm thick, was erected over the section. When the arch was completed the whole eastern periphery shaft could be filled with sand up to the very top. This complicated construction thus played a well-calculated function in the ingenious system designed to protect the burial chamber.

The burial chamber at the bottom of the central shaft contained other features making up part of the sand underground security sealing system. These were funneled apertures in the vault of the chamber's ceiling, which in the course of building had been sealed with plugs of conically-shaped pottery vessels. Only the bottoms of these

relatively thin-sided vessels protruded into the chamber. With the plugs installed it was possible to start filling the central shaft above the vault of the burial chamber with sand. This, however, would have been one of the very last phases in the construction of the tomb. Before this came the minutely thought-out construction of the burial chamber and the no less ingenious stage of lowering the giant sarcophagus into it.

First, at the bottom of the central shaft and at a depth of about 15 meters, foundations were laid for the side walls of the bur-

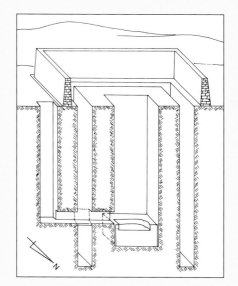

Schematic east–west cross-section of Udjahorresnet's shaft tomb. The dotted line indicates the mudbrick wall in the place where the eastern shaft cuts across the horizontal access corridor and the "drawbridge" was located.

Archaeological work in the huge and deep shafts filled with fine sand is exceedingly difficult and dangerous (photo: Milan Zemina).

ial chamber, which had a rectangular ground plan with an east–west orientation. The walls, made of ashlars of fine white limestone, were built up to a point roughly just under the level at which construction of the vaulted roof of the chamber was to begin. This further stage of building was, however, deliberately delayed and instead the whole of the shaft, including the half-built chamber, which was still open at the top, was filled right up to its mouth with sand. Then a giant limestone sarcophagus of box type was hauled onto the filled shaft. Its lower part had been carved out of a limestone monolith. The lid too was made from a single huge block of fine white limestone 510 centimeters long, 290 centimeters wide and 110 centimeters thick. A horizontal row of hieroglyphic inscriptions with the name and titles of its owner ran around the lower part of the sarcophagus just under its upper edge.

The work in the eastern peripheral shaft above the "drawbridge" (photo: Milan Zemina).

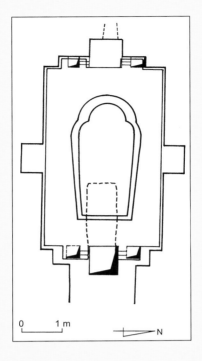

Plan of Udjahorresnet's burial chamber with the box-type limestone and anthropoid basalt sarcophagi.

Inside the limestone sarcophagus another sarcophagus was placed, this time anthropoid in form and made of basalt. This anthropoid, or mummiform, sarcophagus was also huge in dimensions and consisted of two parts, a chest and a lid, the smoothed outer surfaces of which were covered by hieroglyphic inscriptions carved in sunk relief.

When the sarcophagus had been dragged onto the mouth of the shaft, work commenced on removing sand from below, from the half-built burial chamber. This was carried back up through the short horizontal passage and the so-called side shaft. The bulk of the sand thus began to diminish and the huge double sarcophagus little by little sank lower and lower until it finally reached the level of the burial chamber. At this point there was probably some mechanical intervention to slow the descent of the lid and to apply a breaking system in the gap between the chest of the sarcophagus and the lid. The lid of the inner anthropoid sarcophagus had evidently already been slightly raised before the lowering operation began. Finally, the giant double sarcophagus settled on the floor of the burial chamber, and both the inner and outer lids left slightly raised to just the level that would later allow the mummy of the tomb's owner to be slid inside. Only after all this would the ceiling vault be completed.

Finally, after the burial ceremony, the last of the priests leaving the burial chamber would give the order to break the pottery plugs in the funneled openings in the arched ceiling. Sand would then have started to cascade into the chamber. The last operation carried out before the retreat from the sarcophagus chamber to the side shaft, from which the escape route led upwards, was to break down the mud brick vault above the "sand sealing"; sand from the eastern peripheral shaft would then begin to pour down into the passage. In a few minutes the whole underground section with the sarcophagus would be buried. Any subsequent attempt to get through to the sarcophagus was foredoomed to failure, since the sand that would have to be removed to make an entry would immediately be replaced by more sand falling from the upper parts of the shafts. The only possible way of overcoming this brilliantly cunning system blocking access to the sarcophagus chamber was to clear the sand filling from both the central and the peripheral shafts. This was the method which thieves finally hit on when they carried out the first break-in, which, to judge by the remains of pottery, occurred in late antiquity (fourth / fifth centuries CE). At first they tried to get through to the underground section by clearing the eastern peripheral shaft and beginning to dig an access tunnel downwards, toward the burial chamber, in its exposed western wall. Where this route led we do not know. It certainly did not reach the burial chamber. They finally decided to clear the greater part of the central shaft and reached the sarcophagus after breaking through the thick vault of the burial chamber. But were the efforts of the tomb robbers ultimately successful?

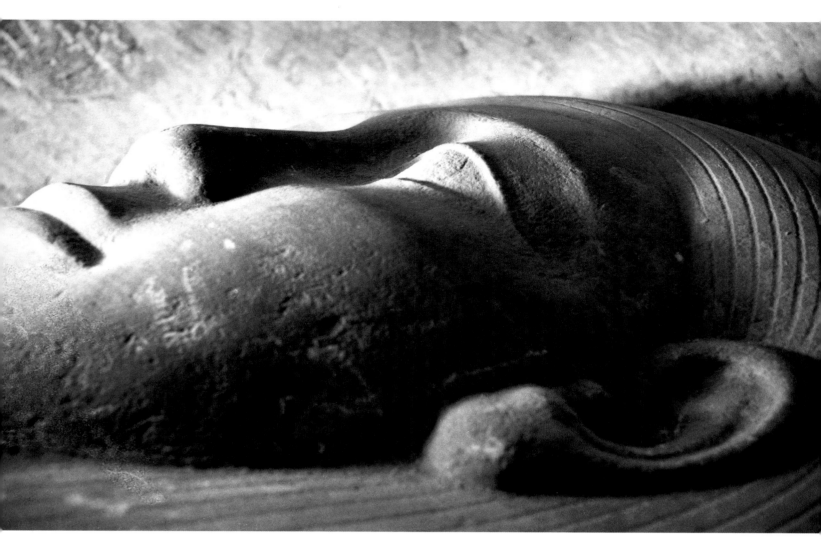

The chamber bore the unmistakable signs of the robbers' activities, including large soot marks left on the vaulted ceiling by torches. There were other black marks on the walls, these ones designed to be here. The hieroglyphic inscriptions on the chamber's side walls were not carved in relief but only lightly drawn in black ink. They contained passages from religious texts and the name and titles of the owner of the tomb.

A large hole had been made in the eastern side of the outer sarcophagus, by which the thieves had got through to the inner, anthropoid sarcophagus. Another, smaller, hole, about 30 by 40 centimeters in size, had been made in the lower part of the lid of the inner sarcophagus. The anthropoid sarcophagus, the lid and chest sealed with red plaster, was empty and its inner surfaces were clean; there was no trace of the physical remains of the tomb's owner. To break a hole in the basalt sarcophagus the thieves had used a fire, which they had kindled at the chosen spot. By repeatedly heating this spot and pouring water over it they weakened the structure of the hard stone so much that they could then easily break a hole in it. This method of breaking hard stone was one that the Ancient Egyptians had been using from the time of the pyramid-builders.

Detail of the face mask of Udjahorresnet from the basalt inner sarcophagus (photo: Jan Brodský).

But had the mummy actually been inside the sarcophagus? It is hardly likely that the resins and oils used in mummification would have left no distinct traces on the inner surface of the sarcophagus. We can also question whether the hole was large enough to pull out the mummy, wrapped as it would have been in linen bandages, without damaging it and leaving no trace. As a matter of fact, not the smallest fragment of the mummy or its linen bandages was found either in the sarcophagus or in the burial chamber. As investigation of the tomb continued the mysteries increased rather than diminished.

As soon as it proved possible to decipher them, the inscriptions on the outer and inner sarcophagi and on the walls of the burial chamber caused amazement. These left not the shadow of a doubt that the tomb belonged to Udjahorresnet, one of the most important and at the same time one of the most controversial figures in Egypt at the end of the Saite Period and the beginning of the Ist Persian Domination, which is to say in the second half of the sixth century BCE. Udjahorresnet had been known to Egyptologists for many years before the discovery of his tomb at Abusir. He was known primarily thanks to the inscriptions on a *naophorous* statue of dark-green slate preserved in the Vatican Museum (inv. no. 196). This statue was probably once a part of the Emperor Hadrian's Egyptian collection in Villa Tivoli. Originally, it may have been located in the main temple of the goddess Neith in Sais. This was a town in the western Delta that, at the time of the Twenty-sixth Dynasty, was the seat of the Egyptian kings. The inscriptions with which it is densely covered are biographical in character and provide very important historical testimony concerning the beginning of Persian rule over Egypt. They were first translated and published with a commentary in the 1930s by the celebrated French Egyptologist, Georges Posener, in a work entitled *La Première Domination Perse en Eigypte* (Cairo, 1936).

From the texts on the statue it appeared that Udjahorresnet was "commander of the foreign mercenaries in Egypt," "commander of the Egyptian fleet," "overseer of the scribes of the Great Hall," and the bearer of many other titles in the reigns of Amasis and Psammetichus III, the last kings of the Saite Dynasty. Surprisingly, Udjahorresnet became a high state official in the administration of the Persian Occupation after the Persian defeat of the Egyptians at the Battle of Pelusium. At this time, in the reigns of Cambyses and Darius I, he even occupied one of the highest offices in the land—the office of Head Physician of Upper and Lower Egypt. This office was far from having only the professional connotations that the name suggests, but corresponded roughly to the position of Prime Minister. This evidence has led some Egyptologists to regard Udjahorresnet as a traitor to Egypt, a man who, though one of the highest-ranking of military commanders, forsook his country and went over to the Persians, ultimately becoming their devoted ally. Other Egyptologists reject the

The celebrated naophorous statue of Udjahorresnet made of black-green slate is preserved in the Vatican Museum collection (no. 196).

theory that Udjahorresnet was simply a traitor and collaborator and view his career in a more positive light. This they base on the interpretation of a fragment of an inscription on a piece of a statue of Udjahorresnet discovered during American excavations at Memphis in the mid-1950s. The inscription appears to suggest that Udjahorresnet enjoyed an extraordinary reputation as a great sage and that his cult flourished at Memphis during the fourth century BCE. In the inscription there is an allusion to "177 years" and this is believed to refer to the time that had gone by since Udjahorresnet's death. It is likewise suggested that the statue of Udjahorresnet from which the fragment came originally stood in one of the Memphite temples where it had been placed at the beginning of the second Persian Domination over Egypt, in order to remind the Egyptians, after more than one and three-quarter centuries, of the memory and services of this important sage and loyal Persian ally. The discovery of fragments of two other *naophorous* statues coming from Memphis indicate that the cult of Udjahorresnet did indeed exist there. The statues were similar to the one preserved in the Vatican Museum.

There is, however, a certain element of contradiction here. This is because while the discovery of the statues points to a Memphite origin, Udjahorresnet's high-ranking titles and functions, referred to in the inscriptions on the statues, are for the main part linked not to Memphis but to Sais. For this reason it was long believed that any search for Udjahorresnet's tomb should be conducted in Sais. Some Egyptologists even thought that he might be buried as far away as Persepolis. They based this theory on an allusion at the end of the biographical inscription on the Vatican Museum's statue disclosing that Udjahorresnet had been summoned to Persia by the Persian king Darius I to help suppress a rebellion in the very heart of the empire using the Egyptian army. The next part of the inscription is damaged or absent but it has been argued that Udjahorresnet died in that campaign and was buried outside Egypt.

Whatever the fate of Udjahorresnet, neither the inscrip-

Miniature faience and wooden tablets forming part of the foundation deposit at Udjahorresnet's shaft tomb. On several of the tables there is a cartouche with the name of Ahmose II (Gr. Amasis), the penultimate ruler of the Twenty-sixth Dynasty (photo: Milan Zemina).

One of the sarcophagi of sacred Apis bulls in catacombs of the Serapeum in north Saqqara. The sarcophagus was broken into by thieves in early antiquity (photo: Milan Zemina).

tions on his statues nor any other contemporary antiquities provide the least explanation of why this high-ranking dignitary should have chosen the southwestern edge of the pyramid field at Abusir, this remote corner of the Memphite necropolis, for his final resting-place. Did he feel politically and socially isolated in view of his close links with the Persian occupiers and therefore had his tomb built apart from the others, albeit still in the Memphite necropolis? Or was the site chosen, on the contrary, so that Udjahorresnet's tomb might in the future become the center of another large cemetery where other high-ranking dignitaries might ultimately have been buried near the great sage? It is possible that the choice of the site was influenced by its proximity to the Serapeum, the cemetery of the sacred bulls in northwest Saqqara, which at the time was an important religious and cult center, not only for the Memphite necropolis but for the whole of Egypt. In the vicinity of the

Serapeum were catacombs where ibises, baboons, lions, and other sacred animals were interred, cult temples, and many other significant religious buildings. The Serapeum is no more than 1,500 meters southeast of Udjahorresnet's tomb. But on the other hand, it is possible that the choice of site was primarily a matter of quite practical consideration. In this case, the determining factor might have been the fact that the geological base was not composed of rock but of thick layers of hardened marl clay in which the daring and architecturally very original plan of the system of shafts surrounding and protecting the tomb's sarcophagus chamber could be carried out. The questions and conjectures surrounding Udjahorresnet's tomb are legion. One cardinal question, however, stands out from all the rest: was the monument found at Abusir Udjahorresnet's real tomb?

Neither in the burial chamber nor elsewhere in the underground parts of the tomb that have as yet been excavated have any of Udjahorresnet's physical remains, or any other evidence proving beyond doubt the existence of a genuine burial been discovered. On the contrary, archaeological research has so far brought to light several facts that provide grounds for caution and reflection concerning his burial here.

The inscriptions on the walls of the burial chamber remained only at the stage of preliminary drawing and were never carved in the relief (sunk relief, rather than low) as must surely have been the original intention and requirement given the standing of the owner. This fact is in striking contrast not only to the size of the tomb and the originality of its design but also to the estimated length of Udjahorresnet's life. As a matter of fact, Udjahorresnet held high titles as early as in the time of Amasis (Ahmose II), the penultimate ruler of the Twenty-sixth Dynasty, and in that time he also began the construction of his tomb at Abusir, as shown by the king's cartouches on the faience tablets from foundation deposits found at Udjahorresnet's tomb. Udjahorresnet's ambitious official career continued under Psammetik III, Cambyses and, finally, Darius I, during whose reign he died in about 509 BCE. Udjahorresnet thus lived long enough (perhaps between 40 to 50 years and, moreover, always in a privileged social position) to have a good chance to complete his tomb in every detail including the relief decoration of the burial chamber.

Surprisingly few objects were found in Udjahorresnet's tomb which belonged to the burial equipment: fragments of the so-called magical bricks from the Nile silt, two miniature models of votive offering trays in blue-glazed faience, pottery (including some imported Greek wares), and so on. In addition to that, only five faience statuettes known as *ushebtis* were found in the underground section of the tomb—surprisingly little, especially for the burial equipment of a magnate and political functionary of Udjahorresnet's importance! For mortuary cult reasons, 365 of the *ushebti* statuettes would usually have been deposited in a tomb, one for every day of the year and, in addition, statuettes of foremen, one for every ten of these statuette servants in the other world. It should be added in this context that three of the five *ushebti* statuettes found were discovered in the sand filling. This had slid down into the underground section from the eastern peripheral shaft in a direction leading from the mouth of the thieves' tunnel. Unfortunately, this tunnel is clogged with sand today and cannot be cleaned out and investigated. But, as has already been noted, it does not lead to the sarcophagus chamber. In a nutshell, neither in the sarcophagus chamber not anywhere else in the excavated part of the tomb has any important component of a burial been discovered; this includes the canopic jars that should have contained the sealed remains of the internal organs removed during the mummifying procedures.

In the rubble and sand that choked the horizontal passage linking the bottom of the side shaft and the burial chamber, two fragments of limestone were found which fitted together. These came from a vaulted ceiling. On the fragments were remains of hieroglyphic inscriptions in sunk relief. Yet nowhere in underground parts of the tomb so far excavated is there a hieroglyphically inscribed limestone arched ceiling or arched portal from which both these fragments could have come. At the same time it is very unlikely that these two fragments were intrusive objects deposited as a result of some strange set of chances and hauled into the underground part of Udjahorresnet's tomb from some other neighboring tomb.

At this point, it should be repeated that the peripheral shafts, arranged in a square around the central shaft, have not yet been cleaned out. This, as has been described, is because of the great volume of sand filling which they contain and the inherent danger that clearing them completely could pose. Given that the periphery shafts are filled with the same laboriously sifted sand, with a volume of several thousand cubic meters, could it be that they function the same way as the central shaft? Are there, then, further undiscovered rooms under these peripheral shafts?

It is rather puzzling that no convincing evidence of a mortuary cult has been found in the vicinity of the above-ground part of the tomb, either. Egyptian history was full of reverses, periods of advance and decline, victories and defeats. New religious ideas developed and some of the old customs would be abandoned. In fundamental principles, however, continuity remained unbroken and one of those principles was belief in a life after death and the duty of ensuring that the dead were provided with a mortuary cult. Yet no mortuary cult site has so far been found near Udjahorresnet's tomb (there is no entrance aperture in the enclosure wall and the cult could have, therefore, taken place only outside this enclosure).

Robbers, as has been mentioned several times, got through to the underground part of the tomb in the face of its builder's cunning security system. They managed to break in several times, first in the late antiquity (fourth / fifth century CE) and for the last time perhaps in the early Islamic period (ninth / tenth century CE). The central shaft and, in part, even the eastern shaft were cleared out by them. The thieves repeatedly tried to get down to the underground part not only via the shafts but in other places as well. It has already been mentioned, for example, that they dug a tunnel in the *tafla* wall between the eastern and central shafts, the mouth of which is to be found perhaps six meters under the upper edge of the western wall of the eastern shaft. Immediately behind the entrance aperture the tunnel divides, one branch leading horizontally to the north and the other turning straight down at right angles. The tunnels, however, have collapsed and are full of rubble and sand, and for reasons of safety cannot be explored. It is nevertheless surprising that nowhere in the part of the underground section yet excavated have their exits been found.

Although they could be further elaborated and augmented, we can now summarize the archaeological discoveries and observations here in terms of two conclusions or questions which appear to contradict one another. First, is the ingenious shaft tomb complex constructed for Udjahorresnet on the southeast edge of the Abusir cemetery a genuine tomb or one that is only symbolic in character? Second, is there, in addition to the excavated section of the tomb, yet another part that has so far not been revealed?

Finding answers to these questions will not be easy. Further excavations in Udjahorresnet's shaft tomb would be not only very demanding but also, and above all, very unsafe and liable to have serious effects on the stability of the whole tomb. Much easier will be the examination of the immediate vicinity of the tomb where other shafts (one such shaft lies close to the southwest corner of the enclosure wall), some of them possibly connected with Udjahorresnet's tomb, may exist. In practical terms, there is also the possibility left open of completing research on the underground part of the shaft complex by geophysical measuring. Even the employment of this method, however, will not be easy under the prevailing conditions. No matter how difficult the circumstances may be, however, the examination of this tomb should be continued so that the mystery of Udjahorresnet's funerary monument in Abusir can finally be unraveled.

A fragment of pottery with a picture of a sphinx was found at the mouth of the so-called working shaft of Udjahorresnet's tomb. Red baked clay with remains of polychrome. 8.5 by 6.5 centimeters. Imported from the Aegean area, end of the sixth century BCE (photo: Milan Zemina).

Egyptian workman
clearing the underground
galleries of Abusir
(photo: Kamil Voděra).

CHAPTER IX

Iufaa—an Intact Tomb!

Archaeological field work is patient and seemingly unexciting labor with only rare lucky finds or, as the Arabs say, the "onion" days which are only rarely interrupted by a "honey" day. The Czech archaeological team at Abusir had an opportunity to realize to its full extent the verity of this saying in 1996 when it succeeded in making its luckiest find so far: the unrobbed shaft tomb of Iufaa. The thrilling story of the discovery, excavation, and saving of the tomb of Iufaa taught the team a lesson about the complexity of archaeological field work and the ever present safety risks entailed in this work. Indeed, the lucky find came perilously close to ending as an absolute disaster.

As described in the previous chapter, in the late 70s the Czech team identified a large Saite-Persian cemetery with shaft tombs in South-West Abusir and ten years later began the exploratory investigation in this area with the excavation of the dominant monument of the cemetery, the shaft tomb of Udjahorresnet. Though very demanding and often risky, the work in the intriguing system of shafts of Udjahorresnet's tomb was successfully concluded in the 1990. The experiences gained by the team during the work in Udjahorresnet's tomb were great and it seemed that a future excavation of any shaft complex would represent no major archaeological challenge for the team. It was to be shown very soon how false this feeling was.

In spring of 1995, the Czech team began the clearing of the second tomb that lay close to Udjahorresnet's monument, on its southeastern corner. Once again a huge central shaft—this one much larger than that of Udjahorresnet—was found. It, too, had been surrounded by an enclosure wall, this one of mud brick. The wall was greatly denuded, but did reveal that it had had niches on its outer sides. Fragments of inscribed limestone slabs found in the area suggested that there had been stelae set within some of the niches at least. There was no elaborate pattern of subsidiary shafts as there had been accompanying Udjahorresnet's main shaft, but there was one subsidiary shaft outside the western enclosure wall of the tomb, and another one to the south. All these shafts had been excavated in the hardened marl clay known as *tafla*.

Both subsidiary shafts were emptied. From the bottom of the western shaft, at a depth of about 22 meters, a short corridor, which went towards the east, was blocked and dangerously damaged, preventing further access. The southern shaft had been badly damaged by robbers. At a depth of about 14 meters, it turned from being a vertical shaft into a passage, which sloped steeply downwards in a northerly direction and seemed to end in the sand filling of the central shaft.

It was then decided that the excavation of the main shaft would have to take place—a difficult and dangerous job in which there were few rewards. The upper part of this shaft—which had also been unearthed by robbers in antiquity—had been badly eroded, and the excavators, directed at that time by Ladislav Bareš, anticipated that they were dealing with a plundered tomb. To their great surprise, however, at the bottom of the main shaft (about 22 meters below ground level) they found a small, intact burial chamber—the dream of every archaeologist! The last intact shaft tomb of approximately this type and date was found more than half a century ago, in 1941, by Zaky Y. Saad in North Saqqara. Needless to say, the Czech team was overcome by euphoria.

The burial chamber was built of limestone ashlars and had a barrel-vaulted roof. It had an east–west orientation and was slightly irregular in shape, due to the fact that it had been built around the irregularly positioned limestone sarcophagus inside. The entrance to the chamber was in its western wall and, at the time of discovery, the entrance was still blocked by the original masonry.

Once this blockage had been documented, it was dismantled, and the chamber itself was entered. Most of the chamber was filled with a huge box sarcophagus, standing some two and half meter high. Between the chamber walls and those of the sarcophagus, there was a narrow passage, in which funerary offerings had been left. The walls of the tomb, but not its ceiling, were densely covered with fine hieroglyphic texts in low relief. These texts were interspersed with religious vignettes of equally fine relief work. The east and west walls were taller than those of the north and south walls, and the tops of them were rounded. There were more decorations on those end walls than on the others. Some sections of the western wall were not in relief; their texts had been outlined in red paint, but they had not been carved. It seems to offer evidence for the western wall having been the last area of the tomb to have been

Face mask of Iufaa's anthropoid sarcophagus (photo: Kamil Voděra).

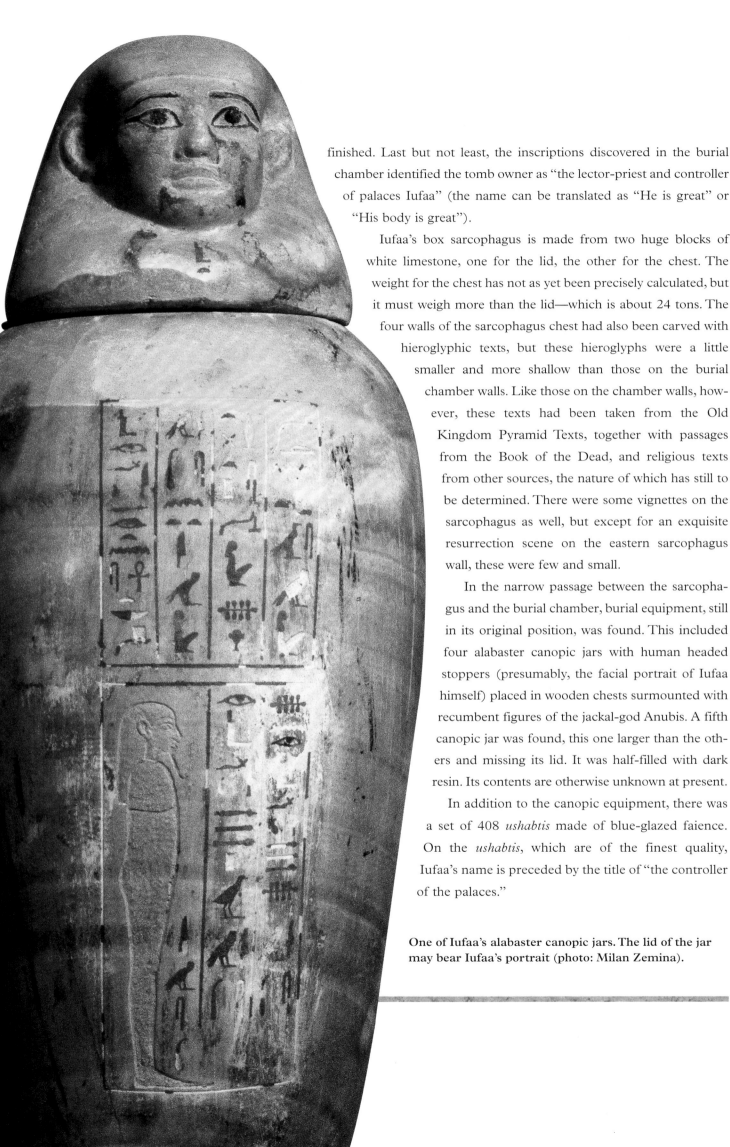

finished. Last but not least, the inscriptions discovered in the burial chamber identified the tomb owner as "the lector-priest and controller of palaces Iufaa" (the name can be translated as "He is great" or "His body is great").

Iufaa's box sarcophagus is made from two huge blocks of white limestone, one for the lid, the other for the chest. The weight for the chest has not as yet been precisely calculated, but it must weigh more than the lid—which is about 24 tons. The four walls of the sarcophagus chest had also been carved with hieroglyphic texts, but these hieroglyphs were a little smaller and more shallow than those on the burial chamber walls. Like those on the chamber walls, however, these texts had been taken from the Old Kingdom Pyramid Texts, together with passages from the Book of the Dead, and religious texts from other sources, the nature of which has still to be determined. There were some vignettes on the sarcophagus as well, but except for an exquisite resurrection scene on the eastern sarcophagus wall, these were few and small.

In the narrow passage between the sarcophagus and the burial chamber, burial equipment, still in its original position, was found. This included four alabaster canopic jars with human headed stoppers (presumably, the facial portrait of Iufaa himself) placed in wooden chests surmounted with recumbent figures of the jackal-god Anubis. A fifth canopic jar was found, this one larger than the others and missing its lid. It was half-filled with dark resin. Its contents are otherwise unknown at present.

In addition to the canopic equipment, there was a set of 408 *ushabtis* made of blue-glazed faience. On the *ushabtis*, which are of the finest quality, Iufaa's name is preceded by the title of "the controller of the palaces."

One of Iufaa's alabaster canopic jars. The lid of the jar may bear Iufaa's portrait (photo: Milan Zemina).

There were many other funerary objects deposited in the tomb cavity: a few pieces of wooden furniture, model items made of faience and copper, miniature stone vessels, inscribed magical bricks in clay (badly destroyed in the damp and humid atmosphere of the tomb), the remnants of papyri inscribed with the Book of the Dead, pottery, some metal scraps, and so on.

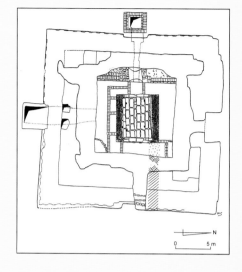

Nonetheless, the euphoria of the initial discovery quickly evaporated when, a few weeks after the spring season ended, it was discovered that the walls of the main shaft were cracking. This was because the excavation of the shaft had removed the protective sand that had maintained the damp underground conditions for so long. While the damp conditions had caused deterioration of the burial goods in Iufaa's tomb, they had also kept the unstable *tafla* moist and relatively firm. Once the shaft had been unearthed, the sunshine and the circulation of the hot desert air caused the *tafla* to dry out. Large parts of the northern wall of the main shaft in particular, but also minor parts of other walls, collapsed onto the burial chamber below. All of a sudden, the team faced a dilemma: either they had to stop the examination of the shaft and bury it under sand again (as recommended by some experts), or an attempt had to be made to remedy the situation. The decision was not easy and, moreover, it had to be taken immediately. After considering all circumstances, it was decided to save the

Horizontal cross-section at the foundation level of the superstructure and a view from above looking down on the burial chamber at the bottom of the main shaft of Iufaa's tomb (by Květa Smoláriková).

tomb, no matter how technically demanding and costly this work might be.

The work that followed was a race against time. The Czech team's architect, Michal Balík, designed an ingenious gabled coffer of reinforced concrete to enclose the entire burial chamber. This was the only way to consolidate the damaged main shaft and save the monument.

The building of the gabled coffer in the desert and, moreover, at the bottom of a huge shaft whose walls were crumbling, brought enormous logistic and safety problems. Every drop of water had to be carried about a kilometer to the site mostly on the backs of donkeys. Thirty tons of steel rods—some of them almost

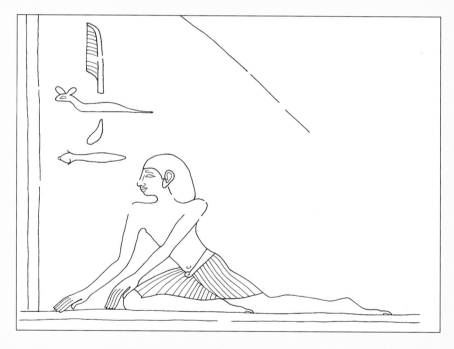

three centimeters in diameter—came the same way, while cement, pebbles, wooden beams, and planks were all brought by tractor across the desert. The sand was obtained from the desert, but the men had to sift it first. In total, about four hundred cubic meters of concrete had to be produced.

Kneeling Iufaa. A detail of the relief decoration on the western wall of Iufaa's burial chamber (by Jolana Malátková).

Once the materials were present at the site, a daily ritual of cement mixing took place at the top of the shaft. The wet cement was then rushed by wheelbarrow to a wide plastic conduit that workmen called the elephant's trunk, which carried the mixture down to the bottom of the shaft, where other workmen manhandled it into position. It is not easy to find the words to describe the efforts and the courage of all the people involved in this project—in particular, the workmen, led by *reis* Mohammad Tallal al-Qereti and his brother *reis* Ahmed. Senior inspector, Mr. Attallah al-Khouly of the Supreme Council of Antiquities supervised all the work and helped to bring about the successful realization of the architect's design. The firm support of Dr. Zahi Hawass, then Director of the Pyramid Zone, was truly invaluable for the success of this demanding project. Thanks to all of these people, the monument of Iufaa was saved.

Only after the construction of the gabled coffer was it possible to resume the archaeological work. The first task to be completed was the tracing of the inscriptions on the burial chamber walls and those of the sarcophagus—in total, about sixty-five square meters of texts and vignettes. The cramped conditions of the burial chamber and the excessive humidity (the bottom of the shaft lies very close to the water table) made the work of tracing physically demanding, but it was completed in the very last moments before the next major stage took place.

The opening of the still intact sarcophagus presented another enormous problem. Eventually, it was decided to raise the huge limestone lid with the help of both mechanical and hydraulic jacks, which first broke the plaster seal joining the lid to the chest, then raised the lid a few centimeters. This delicate operation was achieved by lifting up the lid under the handles protruding from the eastern and western ends of it. Wedges were then inserted one by one into the aperture between lid and chest. Then, when the gap was high enough, these wedges were replaced by blocks of wood. This process was repeated until the lid had been raised to a height of about a meter.

At this stage, four large wooden beams (31 centimeters square and 7.5 meters long), were inserted under the raised lid. Two mechanical jacks were then used to push the lid along those beams and onto the stone and sand platform that had been constructed outside the north tomb wall.

Part of the set of ushebti figures of blue-glazed faience found in Iufaa's burial chamber (photo: Milan Zemina).

The operation to remove the gigantic lid, which had lasted several days, thus revealed the contents of the sarcophagus chest. It proved to be a solid piece of limestone with an anthropoid shaped cavity at its center. Resting inside this cavity was another stone sarcophagus carved from dark-greenish slate. This was almost completely covered with a crumbled layer of mud brick, several centimeters in thickness. The reason for this layer is as yet unknown. Was it intended to imitate the burial in the earth? Or, was it expected to absorb the humidity infiltrating the limestone sarcophagus?

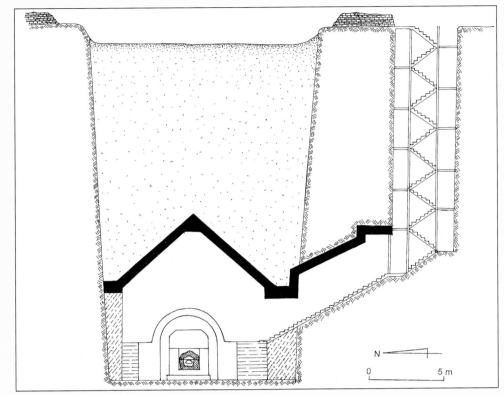

North–south section of the main shaft and the lateral southern shaft of Iufaa's tomb showing the shape and position of the reinforced concrete coffer designed by architect Michal Balík.

The interior of the white limestone sarcophagus was decorated all round its anthropoid sides with finely painted hieroglyphic texts in red, blue and black. At several points, there were polychrome paintings of gods and goddesses. The god Re-Harakhty appears on the eastern section immediately at the head of the cavity of the limestone sarcophagus. The texts, which go down to the base of this inner cavity, were completely obscured by the lower half of the slate sarcophagus. It was wedged into the limestone mold so tightly that, for the time being, every attempt to extract it has failed.

After the mud brick layer had been photographed, measured and drawn, this was

Close-up of a vignette from Iufaa's burial chamber (by Jolana Malátková).

View of the crumbling walls of the main shaft of Iufaa's tomb (photo: Milan Zemina).

removed. It became immediately clear that just before the earthy layer had been deposited on the inner coffin lid, liquid gypsum, mixed with pebbles and large broken potsherds, had been poured all over the lower legs and feet of the anthropoid slate lid, around its head and filling the gap between the slate walls of the sarcophagus and the walls of the limestone cavity. The gypsum had set the carved lid into its limestone bed. In some areas, molten resin had also been poured over sections of the anthropoid lid— it is difficult to tell why, but it must have been during some part of the funerary ritual. All of this had to be removed before the full beauty of the slate lid could be revealed.

The lid was carved in the image of Iufaa as Osiris. He wore the curved beard and a lappet headdress. Around his neck a huge *wesekh*-collar had been carved—a funerary symbol of great antiquity. On his breast there was a carving of a large scarab beetle representing the idea of regeneration in the world of the dead. Below this ran rows and rows of columns containing funerary texts.

The slate sarcophagus lid had to be lifted up by block and tackle. The chains were padded to prevent them from scratching the finely worked lid. This delicate lifting operation took place amidst an assembled crowd of dignitaries, led by Mr. Farouk Hosny, Minister of Culture of the ARE, and an international crowd of reporters, all craning forward to get an early glimpse of the lid and the contents below.

Under the stone lid was a third coffin—this one of wood, covered with painted stucco. It had

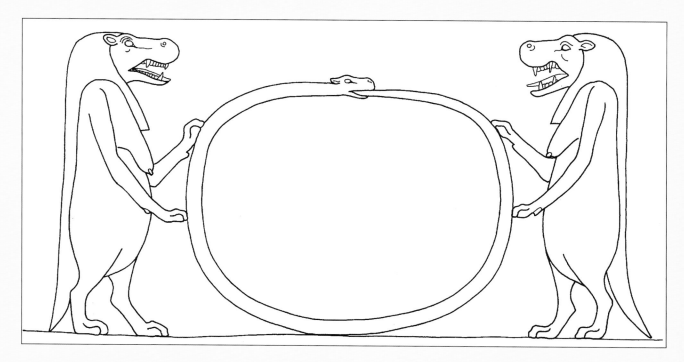

also been carved and painted, but the excessive humidity in the tomb over the centuries had rotted the wood and, when the workmen attempted to lift the lid, it fell to bits in their hands. With the coffin lid being in this terrible state, all feared for the condition of the mummy; as it turned out, those fears were justified. It, too, was beyond saving.

The process of documenting the wooden coffin was then finished and the lid was removed. There was no chance of keeping it intact, but the Czech team was able to copy and photograph the single band of writing that ran down the center of its lid.

The fragments of the lid were then removed and gradually the mummy itself became exposed. It had been wrapped in bandages that had been glued together with resin, forming a stiffened case for the body. In some places, this covering was ten centimeters thick; nonetheless, it had not prevented the deterioration of the mummy, for moisture had seeped into the bandages and reduced the body to a muddy consistency.

The neck and the upper breast of the mummy were again covered by a *wesekh*— collar made of tiny colored faience beads. Below the collar lay a shroud made of blue faience beads. The damp conditions had also affected this garment, for the threads that linked the beads together had rotted away and the majority of the beads had fallen from their original position; many of them had even rolled down into the trough along the sides of the coffin. The tradition of a net shroud of this type is very old. Interspersed among these beads were cut-out figures of several gods: Nut, with her wings outspread, lay across the breast of the mummy, the four sons of Horus faced

Uroboros flanked by two hippopotamus deities. A vignette from the relief decoration of Iufaa's burial chamber (by Jolana Malátková).

Opposite:
Top: Lifting the lid of Iufaa's limestone outer sarcophagus (photo: Milan Zemina).
Bottom: Lowering one of wooden beams through the southern lateral shaft to Iufaa's burial chamber. It was planned that the huge lid of the limestone sarcophagus would rest, after being lifted, on these beams (photo: Milan Zemina).

each other in pairs laid across the upper thighs, while Isis and Nephthys crouched facing each other across the ankles of Iufaa. These positions were probably assigned to those figures because they were considered to be the weak points of the body, and therefore the points most likely to need special protection.

Once the coffin had been lifted out and the floor of the slate sarcophagus had been cleaned, carvings relating to the Afterlife engraved on the floor of the slate chest could be seen. These consisted of short texts and small scenes. Thus it was that Iufaa had been entirely protected by the magical benefit of religious scenes and spells; he had been literally wrapped in texts that were designed to protect him throughout the afterlife.

Iufaa's mummy was taken to the X-ray laboratory at Giza soon after the opening of the tomb. There his remains were x-rayed and studied by the Czech anthropologist, Eugen Strouhal. Early results of the anthropological investigations have revealed that Iufaa was about thirty years of age when he had died, and that the poor fellow had been missing most of his teeth.

Under the mummy's wrappings amulets were unveiled. Although these were not made of precious metals, Iufaa's amulets belong to the peak of amuletic art forms, with no effort spared in making each tiny piece as carefully as possible. Amuletic magic was carried further, with fingers being covered with golden foil, which was not only thought to preserve the flesh, but to transmute Iufaa's body, too.

Iufaa's remains will eventually be returned to his tomb, there to lie once more in the nest of magical utterances that protected him so well in the past. He is not likely to rest in peace, however, for the tomb is designed to be accessible to tourists in the future. Nonetheless, there may be benefits to be had from the stream of visitors we hope will visit this remarkable tomb, for every time one of them pronounces the name of Iufaa, his spirit will thrive in the Afterlife—or so the ancient Egyptians believed.

For the time being, however, the archaeological work in Iufaa's shaft tomb continues. East of the enclosure wall a complex of several rooms, originally roofed with mud brick vaults, was later unearthed. The rooms, in which no remnants of any decoration were found, probably served the purposes of Iufaa's mortuary cult. South of the enclosure wall we found there a descending tunnel ending in the south lateral shaft of Iufaa's tomb. In the tunnel was found the burial of a lady named Imakhkher(et)resnet who, judging by the results of a preliminary anthropological examination of the mummy, was probably a relative (perhaps a sister) of Iufaa. Inside Iufaa's burial chamber the restoration of the texts and vignettes continues.

A *wesekh*-collar made of tiny colored faience beads covered the upper breast of Iufaa's mummy (photo: Miroslav Bárta).

Thus, the secrets of Iufaa's tomb are far from being definitively unraveled. In the western lateral shaft, in the north and west walls, there are sealed entrances giving access to the remaining and as yet unexplored parts of Iufaa's tomb. What surprises may lie in wait for the Czech archaeological team behind these sealed doors?

View of the eastern
facade of Ity's mastaba.
The niched facade was
built in mudbrick
(photo: Milan Zemina).

CHAPTER X

South Abusir:
At the Crossroads
of History

For about two hundred years, the vast Memphite necropolis has attracted the attention of countless archaeologists and it belongs, without any exaggeration, to the best archaeologically examined areas in the world. However, it does not mean—and this has been repeatedly emphasized in the previous chapters—that there are no "white spots" on the archaeological map of the necropolis. Indeed, surprisingly large areas remain as yet unexplored by archaeologists. The same cannot be said, however, for the robbers and their "mapping" of the Memphite necropolis antiquities. Both these statements are illustrated by a large cemetery identified by the Czech team in South Abusir in the late 1970s.

Topographically, South Abusir is an area adjacent from the north to Wadi Abusiri, a shallow valley running approximately northeast–southwest that separates in the Memphite necropolis at Saqqara from the cemeteries of Abusir. To the south, the valley is flanked by the escarpment of North Saqqara on which is situated the Early Dynastic élite cemetery excavated by J. E. Quibell, C. M. Firth, and W. B. Emery. At the foot of the North Saqqara escarpment lies another, socially one step lower, cemetery of upper middle class Egyptians from the same period: that was excavated by H. Bonnet.

Further to the southwest and deeper in the desert lie the royal tombs of the Second Dynasty. Unfortunately, these Second Dynasty royal monuments, the largest of which is *Qisr al-mudir* "Director's enclosure" (this bizarre name, pertaining to Auguste Mariette Pasha, was given to the monument by the local men who worked for him not far from here, in the Serapeum, in the early 1850s) remain as yet largely unexplored. To date, only the underground galleries, which once probably belonged to the tombs of Ninetjer and Raneb, have been examined. Considering all these topographical and archaeological circumstances, there is no wonder that Wadi Abusiri is considered by some Egyptologists to have been the easiest and, in the Early Dynastic Period also the principal access way to Saqqara— a sort of gateway to the then royal necropolis.

In antiquity there was, very probably, a large lake close to the mouth of Wadi Abusiri. As a matter of fact, a lake called by the local people *Birket Mokhtar Pasha*—simply known as the Lake of Abusir by modern archaeologists—existed there as late as the time of the construction of the Aswan dams which terminated the annual floods in the Nile valley north of Aswan. The lake (recorded, for example, on the archaeological map of Abusir by Lepsius's expedition in the early 1840s) was probably a natural water basin, the level of which fluctuated with the height of the Nile floods. Unfortunately, the precise location of the Early Dynastic Period / Old Kingdom lake has not yet been identified. Nevertheless, the results of drill cores carried out along the Saqqara escarpment by British archaeologists within the Egypt Exploration Society's Memphis Project seem to suggest that in the Early Dynastic / Old Kingdom times there were two lakes, one near the valley temple of Unas and the second near the Abusir valley temples. The lakes were separated from each other by a high dry shelf. Possibly, considering the annual siltation and other environmental factors, the Early Dynastic / Old Kingdom lake of Abusir may have lain a bit farther to the east, under the gardens and fields of the present village of Abusir. In any case, the mere existence of two landing ramps—one on the east and one on the south—instead of only one standard eastern ramp in both Sahure's and Niuserre's valley

View of South Abusir from the North Saqqara escarpment. In the background the pyramids of Abusir and, behind them, the pyramids of Giza are visible (photo: Milan Zemina).

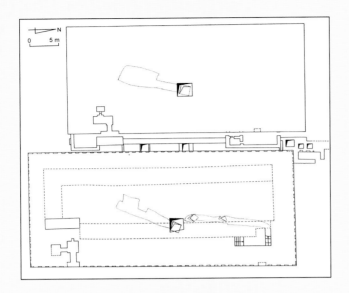

Plan of Kaaper's mastaba (above) and Ity's mastaba in South Abusir (by M. Bárta).

temples seems to anticipate a water way in the southeasterly direction from the temples. If so, it would have been the shortest and the most direct communication between the Abusir pyramid complexes and the large urban center in Memphis, which also included the Temple of Ptah—an institution of vital economic importance for these complexes, as can be inferred from the Abusir papyri.

There are still some other factors to be considered concerning the location of the ancient Lake of Abusir. One of them, for example, is the surprising absence of any buildings on a large raised plateau between South Abusir and the Abusir pyramid field. Did some important installations around the surmised lake (for instance, the royal palaces; see above, p. 150), prevent this prominent place of the Memphite necropolis from being used for building purposes?

According to some Egyptologists, it was just this lake and funerary and religious cults thriving around its western shore that could have given an impetus, at the begin-

Kaaper in the embrace of his consort. A fragment of a scene in low relief from the chapel of Kaaper's mastaba (by H. G. Fischer).

ning of the historic age, to the establishment of the then élite cemetery in the North Saqqara / South Abusir area. As a matter of fact, some scholars incline towards identifying the Lake of Abusir with the mythical lake of Pedju mentioned in the Pyramid Texts—the oldest group of Ancient Egyptian religious texts. It is also thought that the cult of the falcon god Sokar (the god of the dead and ruler of the local cemeteries, and the deity to whom Saqqara probably owes its modern name) arose in close proximity to the Abusir Lake. Moreover, the area with underground catacombs in North Saqqara (and, possibly, also in South Abusir) has been identified with the mythical "Fields of Reeds"—the Elysian Fields of the Ancient Egyptians and the realm of Usir (Gr. Osiris), Lord of the dead. After all, the name "Abusir" is only the Arabic interpretation of the Greek version of the original *Per-Usire*, "the place of Usir's worship."

Though the precise location of the Early Dynastic Period capital of Egypt, *Ineb(u) hedj* ("The White Wall(s)"), has not yet been identified, an opinion prevails among Egyptologists that it probably lay not far from North Saqaara / South Abusir namely, somewhere to the north of the temple of Ptah (significantly in this context, the god worshipped in the temple was called "Ptah-south-of-the Wall," i.e. the White Wall) in Mit Rahina and just opposite the escarpment with the Early Dynastic élite cemetery. Moreover, the results of long-standing explorations have led archaeologists to the ever increasing conviction about a much closer physical association in the Memphite region between the east and west, the capital and the necropolis, than presumed so far. It seems, as the scholars L. Giddy and D. Jeffreys believe, that the Early Dynastic urban center spread along the eastern bank of a natural water basin which facilitated rather than blocked direct communications with the cemeteries lying west of the basin.

The paramount archaeological importance of the South Abusir area was one of the reasons for the rather cautious approach of the Czech team to the opening of the field work there. As a matter of fact, it had originally been planned to begin the systematic exploration of the South Abusir cemetery only after the conclusion of the excavations in and around the so far unexamined Abusir pyramids namely, those of Neferefre and Khentkaus II, and Lepsius nos. XXIV and XXV. However, recent activities from tomb robbers were discovered in South Abusir in the late 1980s, and this accelerated our decision to research in this area. As a matter of fact, a close examination of the site revealed fresh traces of the robbers' digging in two places. One place lay on the top of a hillock in the southernmost outskirts of Abusir, about five hundred meters to the north of the famous mastaba of Ti, the second a bit farther to the northwest. As the excavations were to show fairly rapidly, the first place hid the ruins of Kaaper's mastaba, the other those of the large family tomb complex of Qar.

Shortly before the Czech excavation of the mastaba of Kaaper began in 1991, ten blocks—left on the site by the robbers—had been hastily moved to the storage-rooms of the Antiquities Inspectorate in Saqqara by the inspectors of antiquities. The first finds made in the mastaba of Kaaper, though seriously damaged by the robbers, took the Czech team by surprise: the tomb belonged to a well known Old Kingdom official named Kaaper, a scribe of the king's army. His name and picture are famous in Egyptology thanks to the American Egyptologist Henry G. Fischer's brilliant article published more than thirty years ago. As a matter of fact, Fischer drew remarkably detailed conclusions in his article about not only Kaaper and his career but, at the same time, the original decoration of Kaaper's tomb. The conclusions were based on just a few photographs that he received from Zakariya Ghoneim, the then chief inspector of antiquities in Saqqara. Moreover, Fischer succeeded in finding in various American collections (The William Rockhill Nelson Gallery of Art, Kansas City; The Institute of Arts, Detroit; The Metropolitan Museum of Art, New York) blocks with reliefs that originally belonged to the tomb and were acquired by these museums in the years after World War II.

Even more recently, during preparations for publication of the final edition of a work concerning the archaeological materials unearthed in Kaaper's tomb, more blocks coming originally from this tomb and now scattered in various collections abroad (Foundation Martin Bodmer, Geneva; Bible Lands Museum, Jerusalem; a block published in Sotheby's catalogue, 1996) were identified by Miroslav Bárta of the Czech Institute of Egyptology. Surprisingly, one of the recently identified blocks from Kaaper's mastaba was found more than one kilometer to the south of the tomb by Ian Mathiesson and his collaborators from the Saqqara Survey Project of the National Museums of Scotland when they were surveying the area around *Qisr al-Mudir*. All these loose blocks largely complement the scanty remnants of the original decoration *in situ* in a chapel, the only room besides the serdab in the southeast corner of the mastaba's superstructure.

At the beginning of the Fifth Dynasty, Kaaper, judging by the titles, which represent a major part of the inscriptions so far revealed from his tomb, was an influential dignitary. He was "the inspector of the treasury," "property administrator of the king," "overseer of all works of the king," and so on. Besides these titles linking Kaaper with the top administration, there are, in his titulary, two groups of titles that deserve special attention. The titles of "the herdsman of dappled cattle" or "the scribe of the pasture lands of the dappled cattle" indicate that Kaaper was a high official controlling cattle breeding, which was at that time concentrated mostly in the border regions of the Delta. The other group contains important military titles such as "the scribe of the army," "the inspector of all the bowcase bearers," and "the scribe of the army in *Wenet, Serer, Tepa, Ida*, Terraces of Turquoise, and the Western and Eastern foreign lands." Except for the Terraces of Turquoise, the designation for the turquoise

Opposite:
In the underground section of Ity's mastaba (photo: Kamil Voděra).

mining site of Wadi Maghara in Sinai, and *Tepa*, perhaps a settlement in Nubia, the precise identity of the other localities remains unknown so far. *Wenet, Serer* and *Ida* might have been fortified military camps with Egyptian troops near the northeastern border of Egypt. According to Bárta, it seems likely that these fortresses helped control the routes which connected the Delta with South Palestine and Sinai and which were of vital importance for Egypt. The Syro-Palestinian wine jars found in Kaaper's burial chamber may attest to the tomb owner's administrative engagement in the northeastern border of Egypt. As a whole, the titles seem to indicate that in his time Kaaper was probably one of the key figures in command of the militarily and economically important border regions of Egypt.

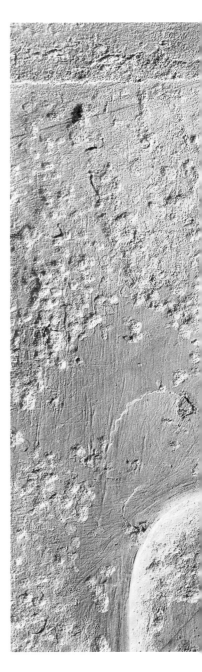

The underground part of the tomb, involving a shaft and a burial chamber, must have been visited and looted by robbers at least twice in antiquity, for the first time at the end of the Old Kingdom and the second time in the Roman Period. The last attempt to penetrate Kaaper's burial chamber can be relatively precisely dated to the mid-1960s, judging by a piece of Arabic newspaper and a fragment of a bakelite lamp found in the shaft. From the few remnants of Kaaper's burial, it is worth mentioning a limestone ear that, very probably, was originally part of the so-called reserve head, a rather mysterious element of the burial equipment whose precise meaning is still being debated by Egyptologists. If so, it would be the second reserve head found so far in Abusir, the first being that found by Borchardt in the Mastaba of Princesses built near Niuserre's pyramid.

To the east of Kaaper's tomb, two large mastabas of a different type and date than the former were unearthed by the Czech team in the 1990s. The owner of the first mastaba, adjacent from the east to that of Kaaper, was identified only thanks to the lucky find of a small, badly eroded libation basin still firmly embedded in the floor in a small chapel in the southeast corner of the mastaba's superstructure. The remnants of an inscription on the basin revealed that the tomb belonged to "the overseer of the two granaries of the Residence, Ity." The superstructure of Ity's tomb has a core made up of pieces of limestone surrounded with a mud brick mantel, the faces of which are decorated on all four sides with recesses.

The substructure involves two burial chambers, independent of each other, planned originally for Ity and his spouse. The northern, corridor-shaped chamber was accessible by means of a twisted staircase, whereas access to the larger, southern chamber was via a vertical shaft. Unfortunately, both underground systems were plundered as early as antiquity. The infrequent finds of pottery help date the monument to the early Fourth Dynasty.

The mastaba of Hetepi can be dated to approximately the same time as Ity's tomb, the late Third / early Fourth Dynasty. It was unearthed farther to the east than Ity's

Hetepi, "the speaker of the king." A detail from the relief decoration of Hetepi's mastaba in south Abusir (photo: Kamil Voděra).

tomb. Hetepi's type of tomb resembles in many respects regarding its structure and building materials used that of Ity. In the southern burial chamber, fragments of a wooden coffin and the skeleton of the tomb owner were found. The remnants of the decoration, including a fine funerary repast scene with inscriptions elegantly carved in low relief on a limestone slab, came to light in Hetepi's chapel, which was located in the southwest corner of the superstructure. These helped identify the tomb owner as Hetepi, "strong voice of the King," "one of the Great Ones of Upper Egypt," and so on.

As previously mentioned, the second place in South Abusir to have been recently damaged by robbers hid a large family tomb complex of the vizier Qar, dating from the time of Pepi I and the early reign of Pepi II. The vizier had quite a curious name, since "Qar" means in Egyptian "the handbag"; nonetheless, this whimsical name proved to be very popular at the beginning of the Sixth Dynasty. The date of Qar's tomb corroborates the theory concerning the horizontal stratigraphy of the tombs in the South Abusir cemetery: it seems that the earlier tombs lie in the east whereas the later ones lie in the west. Moreover, the farther from the Wadi Abusiri, and the deeper in the desert, the lower the social rank of the tomb owners can be expected.

Though already repeatedly plundered repeatedly in antiquity, the inscriptions and other archaeological materials from the family tomb of the vizier Qar brought the Czech team a number of archaeological surprises. Moreover, they introduced the archaeologists to the so far little known and, as it seems, rather turbulent political period at the beginning of the Sixth Dynasty.

A line-drawing of the inscriptions from the false door of Qar (chapel no. 1) (by Jolana Malátková).

Opposite: Qar's false door (chapel no. 2) (photo: Kamil Voděra).

The part of the complex so far unearthed involves, besides the tomb of the vizier Qar, also those of his sons Senedjemib and Inti, born apparently of different wives. (Other members of Qar's family were buried in shafts arranged in row in the western part of the vizier's tomb.) So far unresolved remains the problem of the tomb of Qar-junior, who predeceased his father. As a matter of fact, two chapels in the complex of Qar were revealed, one is undecorated (no. 1) but the other (no. 2) has a nice polychrome decoration in low relief (mostly scenes of bringing the offerings). Each chapel has a false door bearing, besides the funerary formula, the name and titles of Qar. However, the false doors differ from each other in some important details. Except for being more carefully executed, the false door from chapel no. 2 bears not

only more but, at the same time, more important titles. The false door from chapel no. 1 belonged to Qar, who held merely the title of "the 'true' juridical official and mouth of Nekhen" (an old and high juridical title to be perhaps more precisely translated as "speaker of Nekhen /i.e. the Upper Egyptian citadel of Hierakonpolis/ belonging to the Jackal /i.e. the King/"). On false door no. 2, Qar bears the titles of "the vizier," "the overseer of the Six Great Law-courts," and so on, as well as "the

View of Inti's burial chamber with a large limestone sarcophagus which was probably robbed immediately after Inti's burial (photo: Kamil Voděra).

'true' juridical official and speaker of Nekhen" (the latter title being mentioned in the inscriptions on both false doors in a prominent place). Thus the question is: did both chapels, and both false doors, belong to one and the same person namely, Qar-senior (which would be rather unusual) or, did the undecorated chapel, though not directly connected with the burial shaft of Qar-junior, belong to the vizier's son? We shall return to the problem below.

The vizier's burial chamber contained a large, box-shaped sarcophagus in limestone that contained the skeletal remains of the tomb owner. Except for potsherds, nothing has survived from the original burial equipment. However, anticipating the future robbers' activities and the gloomy fate of the physical items of the burial equipment, the walls of burial chamber were inscribed with long lists of offerings needed for the vizier's welfare in the Other World.

Recently unearthed, the tomb of the vizier Qar's son Inti lies adjacent and to the south of his father's tomb. This, too, yielded further important archaeological material. Here again, in the west wall of the chapel, an intact limestone false door bearing Inti's name and titles was found *in situ*. We learn from the inscriptions that Inti was

Inti's consort Merut seated at the foot of her husband smelling a lotus flower. A detail from the polychrome relief decoration in Inti's tomb in south Abusir (photo: Voděra).

A fragment of a limestone block with the sculptures and titles of Meriherishef found in the ruins of Inti's tomb in South Abusir (photo: Kamil Voděra).

"the supervisor of mortuary priests in the pyramid complex of Teti," "the judge of the Six Great Courts," and so on. It seems that in many respects Inti copied the official career of his father. Among the remnants of nice polychrome low reliefs of great workmanship there survived in the chapel a delicate scene of Inti's spouse sitting at his feet and smelling a lotus flower.

Some archaeological finds and observations seem to indicate that Inti's burial chamber might have been plundered, probably with the consent of the necropolis guards, immediately after the placement of the burial in the sarcophagus and the conclusion of funerary ceremonies. To the hasty work of the robbers we possibly owe the finding of a number of less precious items from Inti's burial equipment, such as symbolical miniature offering vessels in alabaster and miniature models of copper instruments.

As briefly remarked above, the inscriptions revealed on the two false doors in

Wall painting with a scene depicting vineyard workers and men trading in a market. Documented in Fetekti's tomb in South Abusir by the Lepsius expedition in the early 1840s. The tomb painting is no longer in existence.

Qar's tomb complex posed a problem the solution of which is not unequivocal. Moreover, provided that both false doors belonged to Qar-senior, the inscriptions might touch, as the Australian Egyptologist Vivienne G. Callender working with the Czech team in Abusir presumes, on an unusual event that happened in the reign of Pepi I namely, a trial of a queen. We learn about the trial from the autobiography of Uni, a high official who lived in the time of Pepi I and Merenre. Uni had on several occasions been entrusted by his lords with some special tasks (for example, a number of military expeditions against the Palestinians, the provision of a rare stone for the construction of the pyramidion of the king's pyramid, the digging of a channel in the area of the first Cataract, and so on). No doubt, however, the most delicate of his missions was the trial involving a queen for some crime (a plot in the royal palace concerning the succesion to the throne?). In the trial, which took place during the early reign of Pepi I and involved the Six Great Courts, Uni was assisted by an anonymous judge, a Speaker of Nekhen. The latter might have been Qar-senior, in which case this event would explain his rapid career. If so, the provision of Qar's tomb might reflect the subsequent upgrading of his social position. In addition, the distinction of "true" being added to his title of "the juridicial official and speaker of Nekhen" would be explained.

As a rule, major finds fill archaeologists with joy and enthusiasm rather than sorrow. However, the latter was certainly the feeling that prevailed in the Czech team at the moment of the discovery of the tomb of Fetekti. Perhaps, it would be more precise to say "the re-discovery," since the tomb had already been unearthed during trial diggings made by Lepsius's expedition in Abusir in 1843. Unfortunately, these diggings were never described in detail nor precisely located on the expedition's archaeological map. The small, late Fifth / early Sixth Dynasty tomb of Fetekti, "the property custodian of the king," was in a way an exception, owing to its very attractive decoration. A few of the wall paintings, such as the vivid scenes of wine pressing, trading in the market, etc., were published in *Lepsius's Denkmäler aus Aegypten und Aethiopien*. Since the 1840s, however, the tomb has been lost. No wonder that its identification in the vast region of South Abusir became one of the objectives of the Czech team, the more so because Fetekti is very probably one of the same-named officials mentioned in the papyri of Neferirkare's temple archive. Eventually, the tomb was identified on the southeast slope of the plateau separating the Abusir pyramid field from the South Abusir cemetery. It was not a happy discovery, however, for unfortunately, all the beautiful wall paintings published in Lepsius's *Denkmäler* were no longer in existence: after the paintings had been copied, Lepsius's expedition apparently left the tomb open and the wind and rain obliterated those fine and detailed paintings.

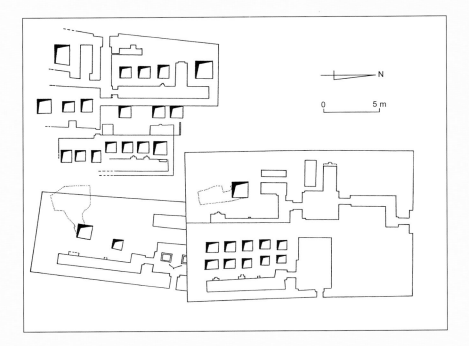

Plan of the lower-middle social strata in the vicinity of Fetekti's tomb in South Abusir (by J. Krejčí and K. Smoláriková).

Fetekti's tomb makes up part of a lower middle class cemetery that dates from the late Fifth and early Sixth Dynasty and extends along the eastern slopes of the plateau between the Abusir pyramids and the South Abusir cemetery. The tombs unearthed so far in this cemetery were entered through a small open courtyard (or, a pillared vestibule as was e.g. Fetekti's tomb). They involve a long, narrow corridor-type chapel and several burial shafts in which the less important members of the tomb owner's family were buried. The owner of the tomb had a roughly hewn burial chamber in the underground part of the tomb. To date, besides Fetekti's tomb the tombs of Hetepi, "the overseer of the storehouse," Isesiseneb, "the juridical official and speaker of Nekhen," Rahotep, "the director of the estates," and Gegi, "the land-tenant," have also been unearthed. Farther to the north, the tomb of Shedu, "the overseer of sweets in the pyramid complex 'Enduring-are-the-(cult)-places-of-Niuserre'" was excavated. Shedu's tomb is adjacent from the west to a large anonymous tomb built of mud brick and dating from the late Third or early Fourth Dynasty. The cemetery around Fetekti's tomb once again confirms how densely built with funerary monuments the whole area, which extends outwards from the eastern outskirts of the desert, from the mouth of Wadi Abusiri as far to the north as Abu Ghurab and,

undoubtedly, still farther on, is. It also shows how complex its stratigraphy in that part of the Memphite necropolis is.

The last decade of the field work in the South Abusir cemetery, briefly reported above, was very demanding (the excavation was immediately followed by large-scale restoration and reconstruction of the tombs) but, at the same time, very exciting, as well. Nevertheless, the quantity and importance of new historical evidence from this so long forgotten corner of the Memphite necropolis is amazing. Though our research is only beginning, South Abusir proves that it indeed represents an important crossroads of Ancient Egypt's history.

Youssef, a conservation specialist from the Saqqara Inspectorate of Antiquities, rescuing the remains of wall paintings in Fetekti's tomb (photo: Kamil Voděra).

The Lepsius expedition on the top of
the pyramid of Cheops: Lepsius' birthday
celebration (Staatliche Museen zu Berlin.
Preussischer Kulturbesitz. Picture reproduced
by kind permission of Dietrich Wildung).

CHAPTER XI

In Search of
Lost Time

L ike so many of Ancient Egypt's illustrious places, into an oblivion from which it seemed there would be no recall. It was an oblivion only confirmed by the activities of generations of tomb robbers, *sab-bakhin,* and stone thieves, whose work of destruction started as early as the end of the second millennium BCE and gradually turned the once noble pyramids into heaps of unlovely ruins. Desert and sand have done no more than mercifully conceal the damage inflicted by man. Nevertheless it seems that the casing of the Abusir pyramids was still largely preserved and the monuments were standing, more or less, in the fullness of their majesty as late as the first century CE. We can judge this by one of the rare written pieces of information about Abusir to come down to us from the ancient world, Pliny's allusion (Hist. 36, 16) to the village of Busiris, whose inhabitants used to climb up the pyramids despite their smooth walls. There is scarcely room for error in the identification of Pliny's Busiris with modern Abusir. Even if we put to one side the etymology of the word Abusir, which is convincing enough by itself, Pliny could not have been referring to any other place with pyramids on the route from Memphis to Giza that he described. The Abusir pyramids did not, indeed, pass entirely unnoticed even in the Arab Middle Ages, but interest in them did not go further than mere mention of their existence in the works of contemporary historians such as Abd al-Latif and Abu Djaafar al-Idrisi.

Interest in the cemetery at Abusir, as in other antiquities of Ancient Egypt, was to be aroused only with Napoleon's campaign at the turn of the eighteenth and nineteenth century. It was only from that time, and hand in hand with the emergence and gradual development of Egyptology, that efforts were increasingly made to investigate

Richard Lepsius.

Ludwig Borchardt.

and study Abusir. Scholars from the scientific commission of Napoleon's campaign, unfortunately without much precision, recorded three "ruined pyramids" near the village of "Abusyr." What especially interested them were the visible remains of the causeways leading to the pyramids from the east and up from the Nile Valley. One remark in their monumental work, *Description de l'Egypte* (vol. 10, p. 455) is, however, very confused. It suggests that one of the Abusir pyramids was made of brick, and this clearly does not correspond to the facts. The error can only be explained by some mistake in the documentation or faulty interpretation of the field records during compilation and editing of the work.

The Englishman John Shae Perring was originally an engineer by profession but Egyptian antiquities, especially pyramids, so captivated him that he devoted the greater part of life to investigating them. It is to him that we owe the first archaeological survey of the Abusir pyramids, which was carried out in 1838. Perring even set himself the dangerous task of unblocking the access routes to the underground sections of the pyramids, and his explorations were not without their dramatic moments. He was given invaluable assistance by the experienced native foreman Abd al-Azdi. Perring was unable to identify the owners of the pyramids with any certainty and so he used "substitute terms" to designate the monuments. The Northern (Sahure's), the Central (Niuserre's), and the Great Pyramid (Neferirkare's). The so-called 'Small Pyramid' represented an error on Perring's part. As was later to be shown, it was not a pyramid but a large mastaba. The plan of the Abusir cemetery which Perring drew up was already much better than the map produced by the scholars of Napoleon's campaign. His first plan of the Abusir pyramids, including basic survey data, was particularly valuable.

Perring's pioneering researches became a solid basis on which the next expedition to arrive in Abusir could rest its work. In 1842, a German-Prussian expedition led by Richard Lepsius, the founder of German Egyptology, came to Abusir, but only stayed there for a very short period; nevertheless, it managed to obtain remarkable results. The archaeological map of the locality prepared by the expedition's surveyors and drafted by Gustav Erbkam became a very valuable and relatively precise aid for subsequent work at Abusir. It contains some inaccuracies, especially in the identification of some ruins as pyramids when in fact they were not and vice versa, but on the other hand, it records some features that have since vanished for ever, such as the Lake of Abusir. The expedition's observations and conclusions relating to the largest of the Abusir pyramids—that of Neferirkare, were to exert a long-term influence on Egyptologists and their ideas about how these monuments, still in many respects mysterious, were constructed. The Lepsius expedition did not carry out large-scale excavations at Abusir, although even the little that its members uncovered here became an important part of Egyptological source material, for example Fetekti's tomb with its wonderful wall paintings.

Bonaparte: Napoleon.

"**Soldiers, forty centuries are watching you!**"

The British MP, Henry Windsor Villiers Stuart, a British parliamentary special envoy to Egypt and an enthusiastic admirer of Egyptian antiquities, conducted work in the Abusir area for a short time during the winter of 1882/83. It is to him that we are indebted for such discoveries as the alabaster altar and alabaster basins in Niuserre's sun temple at Abu Ghurab.

In the early 1850s, Auguste Mariette Pasha, one of the founders of Egyptian archaeology, began his excavations in North Saqqara, in and around the Serapeum. Rather than the Egyptian pyramids, it was the private tombs, the mastabas that attracted his attention—as explicitly emphasized in his fundamental work, *Les mastabas de l'Ancien empire* (Paris, 1883). No wonder, therefore, that he showed little interest in the Abusir pyramids. However, when working in North Saqqara, he extended his excavations further to the north and unearthed several tombs in South Abusir.

In 1893—by coincidence at about the same time as the tomb robbers were making the priceless discovery of the papyri from the archive of Neferirkare's mortuary temple—excavations were started again in Abusir, this time by Jacques de Morgan. French in origin, de Morgan was at that time employed as the head of the Antiquities

Inspectorate at Saqqara. After opening the access to the pyramid of Sahure, he decided to excavate the pyramid designated no. XIX on the Lepsius expedition map although later, finding that this was "only" the mastaba of the Vizier Ptahshepses, he curtailed his excavations after a few weeks. De Morgan also devoted attention to surveying the whole cemetery and then brought together his observations, measurements, and conclusions in his archaeological map of the Memphite necropolis— which naturally included Abusir. One is obliged to add that the older archaeological map drawn up by the Lepsius expedition, which at that time had been available for a half-century and which de Morgan undoubtedly used, is more complete and precise that de Morgan's own.

There are very few archaeologists whose work has won them a name etched deeply into the history of Egyptian archaeology—pioneers who early and accurately anticipated the priorities of archaeological research in their time, and who pushed through new methods of fieldwork, and of studying, cataloguing, and making public the knowledge gathered. Ludwig Borchardt, however, is indisputably one of these. In a way it was a piece of archaeological luck that nobody except Perring with his short-term research had shown any interest in the Abusir pyramids. This meant that an expert of Borchardt's stature could, at the very beginning of the last century, embark on the investigation of pyramids that were relatively untouched by modern excavations. He chose outstanding contemporary German Egyptologists as his colleagues, both for fieldwork and for the study, cataloguing, and publishing of the archaeological finds and information. They included, for example, Georg Möller, Heinrich Schäfer, and Kurth Sethe. The organizational arrangements for the excavations were also on a very generous scale. The Deutsche Orientgesellschaft provided financial resources at a level that no German excavations in Egypt had previously enjoyed. Moreover, in Abusir and the surrounding villages, adequate labor resources were at that time easily available and very cheap. Borchardt could therefore hire what is by today's standards an unbelievably large number of workmen—in several seasons totaling more than 500 people. The experienced foreman *reis* Mohammed Ahmad al-Senoussi was employed at the head of the workforce.

Borchardt started excavations immediately on finishing his archaeological work in Niuserre's sun temple at Abu Ghurab in September 1901. Information obtained from the research at Abu Ghurab led him to regard excavations in Niuserre's mortuary temple at Abusir as the most urgent priority. His decision was influenced by his Christmas visits to Abusir in 1896 and 1898 and the architectonically and archaeologically unique surface finds that he had made on the site of Niuserre's temple. Another factor was, of course, the discovery of the papyri at the Abusir pyramids, since 1893 the subject of very lively debate in Egyptological circles and one which strongly attracted Borchardt's attention. His excavations in Niuserre's pyramid complex took place over a period from the beginning of January 1902 to roughly the middle of April 1904, always in the winter and spring months. Then Borchardt transferred his attentions to the immediately neighboring pyramid complex of Neferirkare. Here, if we leave aside the two small trial diggings of 1900 and 1903 which were influenced by his efforts to identify the place where the *sabbakhin* had found the papyri in 1893, he carried out excavations in the winter and spring months of 1904 and 1907. Borchardt concluded his research at Abusir with unbroken work

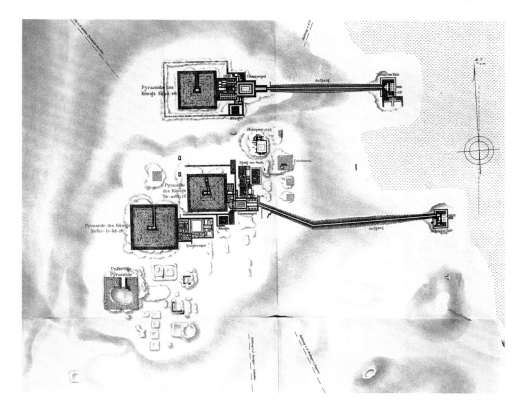

Plan of the pyramid cemetery drawn up at the end of Borchardt's archaeological excavations at Abusir.

in Sahure's pyramid complex from the end of March 1907 to the end of March 1908. Particularly during these concluding phases, he also undertook several smaller trial diggings in other places in the cemetery, such as at the Unfinished Pyramid (Neferefre's) and on the edge of the desert south of Niuserre's valley temple.

Borchardt would give immediate reports on his excavations in provisional form in *Mitteilungen der Deutschen Orientgesellschaft*. He also did not put off, as is unfortunately so often the case in Egyptian archaeology, overall evaluation of his archaeological discoveries and publication of the final excavation reports. These he published in a series of monographs devoted to the three largest Abusir pyramid complexes.

The overall contribution of Borchardt's work to the study of pyramids at Abusir cannot be expressed in a few sentences. One can only, perhaps, emphasize the aspects of his achievement that far transcended the limits of his period and today still represent a standard which many excavations at the beginning of the twenty-first century are a long way from reaching. Borchardt's fieldwork and archaeological publications are pervaded by his ability, so rare, yet so essential in an Egyptologist, to orient himself quickly and surely in the face of a large number of the most diverse archaeological finds and to distinguish between the significant and the inessential in the tangled web of their wider historical contexts. To this day, the imaginative powers that enabled Borchardt to reconstruct the original form of a column, wall or even the plan of a whole pyramid complex from a few fragments arouse admiration. It is no wonder that Ludwig Borchardt, founder of the Deutsches Archaologisches Institut—Abteilung Kairo, and later also of the Schweizerisches Institut fur Ägyptische Bauforschung und Altertumskunde in Kairo, represents a model for the future generations of Egyptologists and field archaeologists.

Vito Maragioglio
(photo:
Milan Zemina).

During his work in the Abusir pyramids, Borchardt was contacted by local people and offered some stone vessels dating from the Early Dynastic Period, which allegedly had been found close to the village of Abusir. The archaeological importance of the vessels gave impetus to the commencement of an excavation at the northern foot of the escarpment, the place where the antiquities were found, where the royal Early Dynastic tombs had been established in North Saqqara. The excavation, begun in 1910 and directed by Hans Bonnet, resulted in the discovery of a large cemetery in which were buried members of the Early Dynastic middle class, socially less important than the élite buried on the top of the escarpment. Both Bonnet's and Makramallah's excavations brought a number of important archaeological materials pertaining not only to the élite, but also to people of the lower social strata in the Abusir necropolis.

After Borchardt's excavations, Abusir again found itself on the periphery of Egyptological interest. Leaving aside a brief excavation conducted perhaps by Ludwig Keimer in South Abusir in the early 1940s (from this excavation carried out near the tomb of Fetekti no report has survived except for few remarks in the *Journal d'entrée* of the Egyptian Museum in Cairo), it was almost fifty years before archaeol-

ogists returned to the Abusir pyramids once more. Then, between 1954 and 1957, a joint German-Swiss expedition spent three archaeological seasons in the ruins of Userkaf's sun temple on the northern edge of the Abusir cemetery. This monument had already been known for a long time and had even been entered on the Lepsius expedition archaeological map of Abusir. The excavations were headed by Hans Stock, at that time the director of the German Archaeological Institute in Cairo, and by Herbert Ricke, the then director of the Swiss Institute for Research into Egyptian Architecture and Antiquities. They worked alongside several other outstanding Egyptologists: Elmar Edel, Gerhard Haeny, Werner Kaiser, Peter Kaplony, Wolfgang Helck and Siegfried Schott. The results of the excavations were something of a disappointment for the German-Swiss expedition, since the whole great building complex of Userkaf's sun temple had been almost completely destroyed in the course of the

Herbert Ricke.

centuries. Nevertheless, thanks to the outstanding professional qualities of all its members, the joint expedition managed to reconstruct from the scanty remains both the original plan of the sun temple and the plans of its later reconstructions.

Though not connected with any excavation, invaluable information on the Abusir necropolis and, especially, on its dominant monuments, the pyramids, resulted from a survey conducted by two Italian scholars, Vito Maragioglio and Celeste Rinaldi. The survey, carried out in the 1960s, resulted in improved plans of the Abusir pyramids and a number of inspiring observations on the Abusir necropolis itself.

In the late 1980s, the archaeological expedition of the Cairo university directed by Ali Radwan began to explore the area to the east of the sun temple of Userkaf and to the northeast of the sun temple of Niuserre in Abu Ghurab. In the former area, a large Fifth and Sixth Dynasty cemetery with mud brick tombs of the members of the lower middle class were revealed. However, in the latter area, near Niuserre's sun temple, the important discovery of an Early Dynastic burial ground with large mastabas, including dummy graves, ritual burials of donkeys, and so on, was made. The very existence of this cemetery, whose future excavation seems to be very promising, clearly indicated that there had been a chain of rich cemeteries stretching towards the outskirts of the desert. They lay between Saqqara and Giza as early as the dawn of Egyptian history, thus anticipating the importance of the area to encompass a few centuries the pyramid fields.

Behind the arrival of a Czech expedition in Abusir at the very beginning of the 1960s lay an interesting and somewhat tangled story that had really begun twenty years earlier. The outbreak of the Second World War had caught the Czech Egyptologist, Jaroslav Černý, in Egypt, where he was taking part in French excavations at Deir al-Medina. He could not return to his occupied homeland and so he lived out the war in Egypt. There was one very important bright side to Černý's involuntary years of exile. They allowed him to devote himself, in the relative calm of the Institut Francais d'Archéologie Orientale du Caire, and of Egypt, to a thorough study of Ancient Egyptian antiquities, both in museums and depositaries and at both famous and lesser-known archaeological sites. Černý visited Abusir as well as other sites and in Ptashepses's mastaba he copied down the inscriptions that he considered interesting and important. During his work he realized how historically significant a person Ptahshepses had been and that de Morgan had only uncovered a small part of a monument that must originally have been much larger. Two decades later he remembered this information in connection with the launch of the activities of the Cairo branch of the Czech (then Czechoslovak) Institute of Egyptology at Prague's Charles University.

In the first years of its existence, the main task of the newly-founded institute was to make a scientific contribution to the international UNESCO rescue projects in Nubia. Although this was urgent and important work, however, it represented only a short-term episode in the institute's planned activity in Egypt. The basic aim was to conduct long-term Egyptological research on chosen archaeological locations in Egypt. On Černý's recommendation, the choice ultimately fell on Abusir. Zbyněk Žába, who had taken on the leadership of research as the deputy of the then already elderly director of the Institute, František Lexa, had taken various additional circumstances into account. Above all there was the fact that Abusir was part of the

Jaroslav Černý and
Zbyněk Žába by a portrait
of the founder of Czech
Egyptology František
Lexa (The Czech Institute
of Egyptology at Charles
University in Prague,
April 1967) (photo: Milan
Zemina).

great and immeasurably historically valuable necropolis of ancient Memphis. It was
also not unimportant that Abusir was near Cairo, since economic considerations were
also factors in the decision.

The circumstances in which Žába started excavations in Ptahshepses' tomb were
not easy. This was because the work of the Czech Egyptological expedition in Egypt
began in two places, Abusir and Nubia, at once. Each of the two research projects was
very demanding in organizational terms, each had its own specific scientific character and required a completely different methodological approach. Yet another com-
plication arose from the fact that the team that Žába had assembled was distinctly
heterogeneous and he was the only Egyptologist among them. Regardless of all these
difficulties, Žába managed to consolidate the position of the Institute in Egypt, to fulfill the scientific tasks allocated to it in the framework of the UNESCO international
rescue project in Nubia and to develop systematic archaeological research in the
mastaba of Ptahshepses at Abusir.

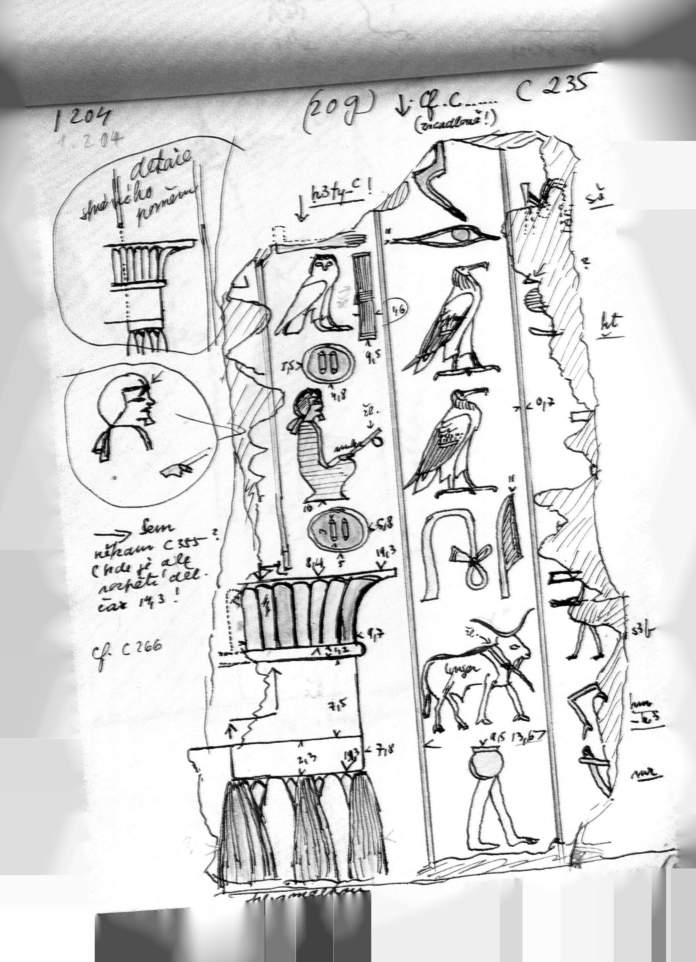

Reis Mohammad
Talaal al-Qereti
(photo: Kamil Voděra).

Opposite page:
A page from Žába's diary
(photo: Milan Zemina).

After Žába's untimely death in 1971 the position of the Czech Institute of Egyptology became ever more complex and difficult, both in Prague and in Cairo. The works at Abusir were suspended for several years and it was only in the first half of 1974 that excavations in the mastaba of Ptahshepses could be restarted. Unfortunately, sudden death had caught Žába just as he was putting together the great stacks of documentation from the excavations and preparing them for publication. It may seem surprising to some that he did not publish interim preliminary reports on his excavations in Czech or international archaeological and Egyptological journals; to those who knew Žába even slightly, however, it is not so difficult to understand. His passion for detail, precision, exhaustive analysis of problems and as far as possible incontestable conclusions were at odds with the requirements of a preliminary archaeological report.

The man appointed to lead the work was František Váhala, a distinguished linguist who had studied Egyptology with František Lexa before the war. Under his direction, the Czech team completed the excavation in the Ptahshepses mastaba in 1974. Unfortunately, however, shortly after his return from Egypt, Váhala died.

Since 1976, the author of this book has continued the work as director of the Czech archaeological excavations in Abusir.

In the mid-1970s, with the end of excavations in the mastaba of Ptahshepses, the Czech Institute managed to obtain the consent of the authorities of the Egyptian Antiquities Organization to transfer research to the southern, archaeologically underinvestigated area of the Abusir cemetery. This new archaeological concession is geographically defined in the north by a line linking Neferirkare's pyramid with Niuserre's valley temple and, in the south, by the shallow valley of Wadi Abusiri which divides South Abusir from North Saqqara.

So far, work has been carried out over eighteen excavation seasons in the new concession in South Abusir. The excavations have been led by the author of this book with the long-term assistance of Ladislav Bareš and Břetislav Vachala, and, in more recent time, by Miroslav Bárta, Jaromír Krejčí, and Květa Smoláriková. Experts in other fields, such as geophysics, anthropology, geodetics, restoration, have joined in the expedition according to need and the specific tasks involved, and students of Egyptology from the Charles University have also participated. In recent years the Czech expedition has also enjoyed close co-operation during excavations with a number of foreign Egyptologists, including the late Paule Posener-Kriéger, Peter Jánosi, Vivienne G. Callender, and others. The foremen of the workmen at the excavations are the sons of *reis* Abdu al-Qereti, the experienced and energetic *reisin* Muhammad Talal al-Qereti and his brother Ahmad al-Qereti. The Czech expedition's archaeological concession in South Abusir, so remarkable in its location and extent, is enabling us to develop broadly conceived and long-term research aimed at providing knowledge and understanding of a number of key questions in Egyptian history. Such questions as the transition from the Fourth to the Fifth Dynasty, the methods used in building the Fifth Dynasty pyramids, the social and economic development of Egypt in the Old Kingdom, and the complex questions concerning the history of Egypt at the time of the Persian domination. It is for the reader to judge how far we are succeeding in this aim. This book is offered as one account which may help the reader to form an opinion.

Reis Ahmad al-Qereti (photo: Milan Zemina).

Detail of a lion head
from the decoration
of one of the alabaster
embalming tables of
the sacred Apis bulls
in Mit Rahina (photo:
Milan Zemina).

Chronological List of Rulers and Dynasties

EARLY DYNASTIC PERIOD
(ca. 3100 to 2270 BCE)

Zero Dynasty

(about fifteen rulers in all)

Scorpion

Ka

First Dynasty

Narmer (Menes?)

Aha (Menes?)

Iti

Djer

Wadj (Djet)

Den

Adjib

Semerkhet

Kaa

Second Dynasty

Hetepsekhemwy

Raneb (Nebre)

Ninetjer

Peribsen

Khasekhemwy

OLD KINGDOM
(ca. 2720 to 2180 BCE)

Third Dynasty

Netjerykhet (Djoser)

Sekhemkhet

Sanakhte

Khaba

Huni

Fourth Dynasty

Sneferu

Khufu

Djedefre (Djedefre)

Khafre

Baka

Menkaure

Shepseskaf

Fifth Dynasty

Userkaf

Sahure

Neferirkare

Neferefre

Shepseskare

Niuserre

Menkauhor

Djedkare

Unas

Sixth Dynasty

Teti

Userkare

Pepi I

Merenre I (Antiemsaf I)

Pepi II

Merenre II (Antiemsaf II)

Nitocris (uncertain)

FIRST INTERMEDIATE PERIOD
(ca. 2180 to 1991 BCE)

Seventh/Eighth Dynasties

Ibi

Neferkare Nebi

(In all, some seventeen less important kings who reigned only a short time)

Ninth/Tenth Dynasties

(About eighteen less important kings, some of whom bore the name Khety)

Merikare

Eleventh Dynasty
(first half)

(Mentuhotep I)

Antef I

Antef II

Antef III

Source: Donald Redford, editor, *The Oxford Encyclopedia of Ancient Egypt* (Cairo: Cairo University Press, 2001).

MIDDLE KINGDOM
(1991 to ca. 1759 BCE)

Eleventh Dynasty
(second half)
Mentuhotep II
Mentuhotep III
Mentuhotep IV

Twelfth Dynasty
Amenemhet I
Senusret I
Amenemhet II
Senusret II
Senusret III
Amenemhet III
Amenemhet IV
Nefrusebek

SECOND INTERMEDIATE PERIOD
(ca. 1759 to ca. 1539 BCE)

Thirteenth Dynasty
(Several dozen less important
kings, some of whom bore the
name Sebekhotep)
Khendjer
Ameny Kemau
Auibre Hor

Fourteenth Dynasty
Nehesi

Fifteenth Dynasty
(Seven kings altogether)
Sebekemsaf II
Antef VI
Seqenenre
Kamose

NEW KINGDOM
(ca. 1539 to 1076 BCE)

Eighteenth Dynasty
Ahmose I
Amenhotep I
Thutmose I
Thutmose II
Hatshepsut
Thutmose III
Amenhotep II
Thutmose IV
Amenhotep III
Amenhotep IV / Akhenaton
Smenkhkare
Tutankhamen
Ay
Horemheb

Nineteenth Dynasty
(Ramesside period)
Ramses I
Seti I
Ramses II
Merneptah
Seti II
Amenmeses
Siptah
Tausert

Twentieth Dynasty
Setnakht
Ramses III
Ramses IV
Ramses V
Ramses VI
Ramses VII
Ramses VIII
Ramses IX
Ramses X
Ramses XI

THIRD INTERMEDIATE PERIOD
(ca. 1076 to 712 BCE)

Twenty-first Dynasty
Smendes
Amenemnesu
Psuennes I
Amenemope
Osokhor
Siamon
Psusennes II

Twenty-second Dynasty
(Libyan)
Sheshonk I
Osorkon I
Sheshonk II
Takelot I
Osorkon II
Takelot II
Sheshonk III
Pemu
Sheshonk V
Osorkon IV

Twenty-third Dynasty
(Libyan)
Petubastis I
Sheshonk IV
Osorkon III
Takelot III
Rudjamun
Iupet II

Twenty-fourth Dynasty
Tefnakht
Bokhoris

LATE PERIOD
(ca. 712 to 332 BCE)

Twenty-fifth Dynasty
(Cushite)
Kashta
Piye
Shabaka
Shabataka
Taharqa
Tanutamon

Twenty-sixth Dynasty
(Nekho I)
Psammeticus I
Nekho II
Psammeticus II
Apries
Ahmose II (Amasis)
Psammeticus III

Twenty-seventh Dynasty
(first Persian Period)
Cambyses
Darius I
Xerxes I
Artaxerxes I
Darius II

Twenty-eighth Dynasty
Amyrtaeus
Twenty-ninth Dynasty
Neferites I
Psammythis
Achoris

Thirtieth Dynasty
Nektanebo I
Takhos
Nektanebo II

Thirty-first Dynasty (second Persian Period)
Artaxerxes III
Arses
Darius III

Ptolemaic Period (332 to 30 BCE)

Roman Period (30 BCE. to 395 CE)

Byzantine Period (395 CE to 642 CE)

Arab conquest of Egypt (642 CE)

Select Bibliography

Bareš, L., *Abusir IV. The Shaft Tomb of Udjahorresnet at Abusir*, Praha 1999.

Bárta, M., *Abusir V. The Cemeteries of Abusir South* I, Praha 2001.

Bissing, F. W. von (ed.), *Das Re-Heiligtum des Königs Ne-woser-re (Rathures)*. I. *Der Bau* (L. Borchardt), Berlin 1905; II. *Die kleine Festdarstellung* (H. Kees), Leipzig 1923; III. *Die Grosse Festdarstellung* (H. Kees), Leipzig 1928.

Bonnet, H., *Ein frühgeschichtliches Gräberfeld bei Abusir*, Leipzig 1928

Borchardt, L., *Das Grabdenkmal des Königs Ne-user-re'*, Leipzig 1907

Borchardt, L., *Das Grabdenkmal des Königs Nefer-ir-ke3-re'*, Leipzig 1909

Borchardt, L., *Das Grabdenkmal des Königs Sahure-re'* I. *Der Bau*, Leipzig 1910; II. *Die Wandbilder*, Leipzig 1913.

Edel, E., Wenig, S., *Die Jahreszeitenreliefs aus dem Sonnenheiligtum des Königs Ne-user-re*, Berlin 1974.

Krejčí, J., Bárta, M. (eds.), "Abusir and Saqqara in the Year 2000," in: *Archiv orientálni. Supplementa* IX, Praha 2000.

Lepsius, K. R., *Denkmäler aus Aegypten und Aethiopien*, Abth. 1–6, Bd. 1–12, Berlin 1849–1856.

Lepsius, K. R., *Denkmäler aus Aegypten und Aethiopien–Text* I–V, Leipzig 1897–1913.

Maragioglio, V., Rinaldi, C., *L'architettura delle piramidi menfite*. VII–*Text*, *Plates*, Rapallo, 1970.

Morgan, J. de, "Découverte du Mastaba du Ptah-chepsés dans la nécropole d'Abousir," in: *Revue d'archéologique*, 3 éme série–t. XXIV (Janvier–Juin 1894), Paris 1894, pp. 18–33.

Perring, J. S., *The Pyramids of Gizeh, from actual survey and measurement*. Part III, London 1842, pp. 5–9.

View of Kom al-Nawa in the early morning. Mit Rahina (photo: Milan Zemina).

Ricke, H. (ed.), *Das Sonnenheiligtum des Königs Userkaf*.

I. "Der Bau," in *Beiträge zur ägyptischen Bauforschung und Altertumskunde* 7, Kairo 1965.

II. "Die Funde," in *Beiträge zur ägyptischen Bauforschung und Altertumskunde* 8, Wiesbaden 1969.

Schäfer, H., *Priestergräber und andere Grabfunde vom Ende des Alten Reiches bis zur Griechischen Zeit von Totentempel des Ne-user-re*, Leipzig 1908.

Verner, M., *Abusir I. The Mastaba of Ptahshepses. Reliefs* I, Prague 1977.

Verner, M., *Abusir II. Die Baugraffiti der Ptahschepses Mastaba*, Praha 1992.

Verner, M., *Abusir III. The Pyramid Complex of Khentkaus*, Praha 1995.

Verner, M., *Forgotten Pharaohs, Lost Pyramids. Abusir*, Praha 1994.

Verner, M. *The Pyramids*, New York 2001, pp. 280–321.

Verner, M., Callender, V. G., *Abusir VI. Djedkare's Family Cemetery*, Praha 2002

Vyse, H., *Operations carried at the pyramids of Gizeh in 1837, with an account of a voyage into Upper Egypt, and an appendix*, London 1842, pp. 12–37.

For a detailed Egyptological bibliography relating to Abusir, see B. Porter, R. Moss, J. Málek, *Topographical Bibliography of Ancient Egyptian Hieroglyphic Texts, Reliefs, and Paintings. III. Memphis*. Pt. 1, Oxford 1974 (2nd ed.), pp. 324–348. For the most up to date bibliography of papers and monographs published by the members of the Czech archaeological expedition to Abusir, see M. Bárta, "The Czech Institute of Egyptology. Bibliography 1958–1998," in *ArOr* 66, Praha 1998, pp. 17–26.

Index

Egyptian, Greek, and Latin names are in italics.

Personal Names

Abd al-Azdi 226
Abd al-Latif 225
Ahmose II (Gr. Amasis) 186, 188, 189
Akhenaten 9
Altenmuller, Hartwig 100
Amenemhet III 20
Amenhotep II 7
Amon 7
Amr Ibn al-Aas 10
Ankhaf 29
Ankhmahor 39
Anubis 196
Apis 7, 188
Apophis 69
Apries 7, 9
Atum 68, 69

Balík, Michal 197, 200
Bareš, Ladislav 194, 236
Bárta, Miroslav 212, 214, 236
Bedouins 48
Benet 144
Bissing, Friedrich Wilhelm von 77, 79, 137
Bonnerot, Louis 139
Bonnet, Hans 41, 207, 230
Borchardt, Ludwig 42, 44, 49, 77f., 97, 100, 114, 120, 140, 172, 226, 228–30

Callender, Vivienne Gae 2, 221, 236
Cambyses 186
Capart, Jean 11
Cenival, Jean Louis de 141

Černý, Jaroslav 141, 232, 233

Darius I 186f.
Djedefre 27f., 89
Djedi 70f.
Djedkare 33, 64, 84, 131, 142, 149
Djoser 16, 32, 68, 71

Edel, Elmar 231
Emery, Walter Brian 15, 207
Erbkam, Gustav 227
Erman, Adolf 14

Fetekti 43, 221
Firth, Cecil Mallony 207
Fischer, Henry George 212

Gegi 222
Ghazouli, Edouard 58, 101
Ghoneim, Zakariya 212
Giddy, Lisa 211

Haaibre 9
Hadrian 186
Haremheb 49
Hassan, Selim 29, 93, 96f., 106, 140
Hathor 7, 75, 142
Hawass, Zahi 25, 31, 198

Hedjetnub 64
Helck, Wolfgang 231
Hemakhty 166
Herodotus 7
Hetepi 215f.
Holscher, Uvo 92
Horus 28f., 213
Hosny, Farouk 202

al-Idrisi, Abu Djaafar 225
Idu 64
Iput 39
Inherkhau 69
Inti 43, 219
Irukaptah 36
Ity 206, 210, 212, 214
Iufaa 43, 193–205

Jánosi, Peter 236
Jeffreys, David 211
Jéquier, Gustav 39
Junker, Hermann 29

Kaaper 43, 210–14
Kahotep 166
Kaiser, Werner 42, 83, 231
Kakherptah 27
Kaplony, Peter 231
Keimer, Louis 231
Khaba 16
Khafini 166
Khafre (Gr. *Chephren*) 27–29, 89
Khamerernebty 162, 166, 168, 173, 175
Khasekhemwy 16
Khekeretnebty 63f., 146
Khentkaus I 55, 92f., 95f., 106, 108, 140
Khentkaus II 43, 50, 54f., 58, 62, 64, 95–109, 121, 142, 146f., 150, 211
Khenu 166
Khepre 69
Khouly, Attallah 198
Khnumhotep 37, 154
Khuiankh 133
Khufu (Gr. *Cheops*) 11, 25, 28f., 70f., 81, 172, 221
Khufukhaf 29
Krejčí, Jaromír 2, 236

Labrousse, Audron 39
Lauer, Jean-Phillip 85
Leclant, Jean 39
Lehner, Mark 31

Lepsius, Richard Karl 43, 50, 64, 95, 120, 153, 211, 222, 224, 226f., 232f.
Lexa, František 232, 233, 236

Maat 69
Makramallah, Rizkallah Naguib 41, 230
Malátková, Jola 2
Maragioglio, Vito 49, 52, 230, 231
Mariette, August 29, 207, 227
Maspero, Gaston 139
Mathiesson, Ian 212
Mendelssohn, Kurt 21
Meni 5
Menkauhor 33, 59, 84
Menkaure (Gr. *Mykerinos*) 29, 31, 55, 75, 89, 95f.
Merenptah 7
Merenre 221
Mereruka 39
Meriherishef 220
Mernefu 64
Merut 219
Moller, Georg 228
Morgan, Jacques de 154, 168, 227f., 232

Napoleon 225–27
Nebka 70
Nebre 68
Nefer 37
Neferefre 33, 43, 55, 58, 62, 64, 78, 108–33, 148–50, 211
Neferirkare 21, 33, 43, 48–62, 70, 75–85, 97, 100f., 108–14, 118, 138, 142, 144–51, 222, 226f., 229, 236
Neferka 68
Neferkhanebty 50
Neferre 54
Nefertem 7
Neith 39, 186
Nekhbet 48
Netjerikhet 16
Netjerirenre 50, 108
Neserkauhor 64
Niuserre 33, 43, 55, 58–62, 76–85, 102, 108, 122f., 130, 137, 151, 155, 166, 168, 173, 226–29, 232
Nyankhnum 37

Osiris 11, 202

Pepi I 11, 221
Pepi II 39, 131, 142
Perring, John Shae 101, 138, 226
Pliny 225
Posener, Georges 139, 136
Posener-Kriéger, Paule 111, 138, 141, 145, 147, 236
Psammetichus 186
Ptah 6f., 10, 16, 149, 210

Ptahhotep 36
Ptahshepses 1, 39, 43, 83, 85, 109, 154–75, 228, 232

Qar 43, 216, 219, 221
al-Qereti, Abdu 155
al-Qereti, Ahmad 198, 236
al-Qereti, Mohammad Talaal 198, 235f.
Quibell, J. F. 207

Radjedef 23
Radwan, Ali 41, 232
Rahotep 222
Ramesses II 7
Re 42, 68f., 71, 75, 86, 112, 142
Re-Harakhty 68, 200
Reisner, George Andrew 29, 93
Ricke, Herbert 48, 231
Rinaldi, Celeste 49, 52, 231
Rudjdjedet 100

Saad, Zaky Youssef 194
Sahure 33, 39, 42-62, 70, 82–84, 97, 100, 108, 112, 118, 140, 151, 155, 172, 226, 228f.
Sakhmet 7
Schafer, Heinrich 138
Schott, Siegfried 231
Sekhemkhau 54, 58, 122
Selket 144
Senedjemib 68
Senedjemib Inty 29
al-Senoussi, Mohammad Ahmad 228
Seshat 151
Sethe, Kurt 140
Shedu 43, 222
Shepseskaf 11, 29, 32, 75, 89, 93, 96f., 109
Shepseskare 54, 58, 111
Sheshonq I 9
Smoláriková, Květa 236
Sneferu 11, 20f., 24f., 70, 89

Sokar 142
Sopdu 131
Stadelmann, Rainer 84
Stock, Hans 231
Strouhal, Eugen 205
Stuart, Henry Windsor Villiers 227

Teti 142, 220
Thamphthis 109
Ti 33, 84, 211

Udjahorresnet 43, 181–91
Udjebten 39
Unas 33, 37, 44, 142
Uroboros 203
Userkaf 32, 42f., 59, 70f., 74–85, 100, 109, 231f.

Vachala, Břetislav 236
Váhala, František 236
Vikentiev, Vladimir 96
Voděra, Kamil 2
Vymazalová, Hana 2

Wadjet 48, 105, 142
Wellner, Luděk 2
Werbrouck, Marcelle 11
Westcar, Henry 70f.

Žába, Zbyněk 155, 168, 232, 233, 235f.

Place Names

Abu Ghurab 41, 76–85, 137f., 227f., 232
Abu Rawash 28, 154
Abydos 15
Aswan 208

Babylon 10
Birket Mokhtar Pasha 208
Bulaq 139
Busiris 225

Dahshur 11, 20, 81, 24f., 59
Deir al-Medina 69

Fayyum 11, 221f.

Giza 1, 11, 24f., 27-32, 55, 71, 75f., 108, 137, 139, 154, 225, 232

Heliopolis 42, 59, 69, 71, 113
Hierakonpolis 219
Hikuptah 7
Hutkaptah 7

Ida 214
Ineb(u)-hedj 5, 211
Iunu 69, 113

Kom al-Fakhry 7, 10
Kom al-Rabia`a 6

Lake of Abusir 43, 211, 227
Louvre 139

Meidum 11, 16, 21, 29, 39
Men-nefer 11
Men-nefer-Pepi 11
Memphis 1–39, 186, 225, 233
Mit Rahina 5–10, 211
Moqattam 14

Nekhen 71, 219, 221f.
Nubia 214

Palestine 214
Pelusium 186
Per-Usire 211

Sais 186
Sakhebu 70
Saqqara 1, 11, 15f., 32, 37, 59, 71, 75,
    142, 207, 211f., 232
Seila 24
Serer 212, 214
Sinai 214

Tell al-Ruba`a 141
Tepa 212, 214
Terraces of Turqoise 212, 214

Umm al-Qaab 15

Wadi Abusiri 41, 208, 216, 236
Wadi Maghara 214
Wenet 212, 214

Zawiyet al-Aryan 16